India's Industrial Rise

India's Industrial Rise

A Transformative Journey

Maria. M

UNIEK ENTERPRISES

Contents

INDEX

Chapter 7: Technology and Innovation

Chapter 8: The Future of Indian Industry

Chapter 1

Introduction

In the records of worldwide monetary history, India's modern ascent remains as a demonstration of the extraordinary force of constancy, flexibility, and development. The subcontinent's excursion from an overwhelmingly agrarian economy to a prospering modern force to be reckoned with is a convincing story that exemplifies the hardships, the forward leaps and misfortunes, and the commitment and difficulties of a country on the move. As the world's second-most crowded country, India's industrialization interaction has critical ramifications for its 1.4 billion residents as well as for the worldwide monetary scene.

The account of India's modern rising is a complex trap of verifiable, social, and financial strings that have formed the country's direction. An excursion traverses hundreds of years, drawing from the illustrations of provincial oppression, the yearnings of post-freedom country building, and the contemporary powers of globalization. To comprehend this multi-layered change, we should dig into the past and follow the underlying foundations of India's modern turn of events.

India's tryst with industrialization started some time before the nation acquired autonomy from English frontier rule in 1947. The early history of Indian industry can be followed back to the Indus Valley Development, one of the world's most established metropolitan habitats. It thrived around 2600 BCE and included modern metropolitan preparation, normalized loads and measures, and an economy that depended on agribusiness, creature cultivation, and, somewhat, fabricating.

Nonetheless, India's modern ability wound down over hundreds of years because of different verifiable elements, including the decay of native assembling during the Mughal Realm and the manipulative monetary strategies of English expansionism. The English East India Organization's coming in the seventeenth century denoted a critical defining moment in India's financial history. Throughout the long term, the English took advantage of India's assets, deterred native enterprises, and laid out a provincial economy that principally served the interests of the

English Realm. India turned into a provider of natural substances, while English fabricated merchandise overwhelmed the Indian market.

The post-freedom time frame, set apart by the introduction of the Republic of India in 1947, brought reestablished trust for modern turn of events. Pioneers like Jawaharlal Nehru, the nation's most memorable Top state leader, imagined a cutting edge, industrialized India. Nehru's vision was exemplified in the "Five-Year Plans," which established the groundwork for the nation's industrialization. These plans stressed the significance of confidence and native modern turn of events.

The Green Unrest of the 1960s and 1970s, with its emphasis on working on horticultural efficiency, assumed a urgent part in India's modern process. It changed the country's farming area as well as laid the preparation for a thriving food-handling industry. At the same time, the nation put resources into weighty enterprises, like steel, coal, and power, making way for an independent modern base.

One of the most striking examples of overcoming adversity in India's modern process is the data innovation (IT) and programming administrations area. During the 1990s, India immediately jumping all over the chance introduced by the worldwide innovation upheaval, utilizing its immense pool of talented experts to turn into a worldwide center for IT administrations. Organizations like Infosys, Wipro, and Goodbye Consultancy Administrations (TCS) arose as industry pioneers, giving programming arrangements and administrations to clients around the world. The IT business supported India's financial development as well as assisted the country with earning respect as a worldwide mechanical force to be reckoned with.

India's modern ascent has been supported by its segment profit - a youthful and developing populace with a significant labor force. This segment advantage, when joined with a quickly extending working class and expanded urbanization, has filled homegrown utilization, subsequently drawing in unfamiliar financial backers and worldwide companies. The administrations area, enveloping IT, business process re-appropriating, medical services, and training, has encountered huge development, adding to India's monetary broadening.

The auto business is one more imperative part of India's modern scene. With the foundation of notable Indian organizations like Goodbye Engines and Mahindra and Mahindra, and the section of worldwide goliaths like Suzuki, Honda, and Hyundai, India has developed into one of the world's biggest auto markets. The area has seen significant headways in innovation, plan, and creation processes, driving homegrown interest as well as commodities to different nations.

India's drug industry is one more prominent example of overcoming adversity. The nation is a key part in the worldwide drug market, giving reasonable nonexclusive medications to a large number of individuals all over the planet. The area's development is credited to its vigorous innovative work capacities, administrative changes, and a gifted labor force. The drug business is a demonstration of India's obligation to development and its capacity to adjust to developing worldwide business sectors.

In any case, India's modern process isn't without its difficulties. Foundation bottlenecks, administrative formality, and administrative intricacies have presented obstacles to consistent business activities. The nation has been wrestling with issues like land securing and work changes, which have been the subject of broad discussion and conversation. Additionally, monetary imbalance, local inconsistencies, and natural worries keep on being major problems that should be tended to as India propels mechanically.

India's modern ascent has been set apart by the two accomplishments and difficulties, and the country's way ahead will undoubtedly be a nuanced one. As the world advances into the computerized age and stands up to issues connected with environmental change, India's industrialization cycle should adjust and develop. Clean energy and supportable practices are becoming vital, and the country is progressively zeroing in on environmentally friendly power sources to diminish its carbon impression.

1.1 Setting the Stage: India's Historical Context

To comprehend India's contemporary modern ascent, it is basic to dig into its rich authentic setting, as the country's excursion from old human advancement to the current day is a many-sided woven artwork of culture, success, and change. India's set of experiences is a unique continuum that has significantly molded its financial, social, and political scene. From the antiquated Indus Valley Human advancement to the periods of strong domains, the difficulties of expansionism, and the intricacies of post-autonomy country fabricating, this verifiable background establishes the groundwork for appreciating India's modern development.

The foundations of India's development run profound, with the Indus Valley Human advancement being one of the world's most seasoned metropolitan communities. Thriving around 2600 BCE, it displayed astounding advances in metropolitan preparation, exchange, and innovation. In any case, it progressively blurred into lack of clarity, clearing a path for a progression of realms and realms that would administer the subcontinent over centuries.

One of the most noticeable old realms was the Maurya Domain, which rose to control in the fourth century BCE. Under the initiative of Ashoka the Incomparable, this domain saw critical regional extension and the dispersal of Buddhism across the district. The ensuing Gupta Domain, around the fourth to sixth hundreds of years CE, is in many cases viewed as a brilliant period of Indian history, described by a thriving economy, craftsmanship, writing, and logical accomplishment.

The appearance of Islamic lines, especially the Mughals in the sixteenth 100 years, denoted another section in India's set of experiences. The Mughal Domain brought building wonders, social combination, and a flourishing economy, further improving India's job in the worldwide exchange organization. The Mughals addi-tionally added to the improvement of India's agrarian economy, presenting new yields and cultivating strategies that had enduring effects.

Be that as it may, as time elapsed, India experienced influxes of unfamiliar success and imperialism. The English East India Organization's appearance in the seventeenth century started a time of English decide that would keep going for almost two centuries. The pioneer period essentially changed the Indian scene, changing the country into a provider of unrefined components for English en-terprises. India's distinctive and native assembling declined as English produced merchandise overwhelmed the nearby market, prompting a monetary lopsidedness that would significantly influence India's future industrialization.

The battle for freedom from English provincial rule, drove by notable figures like Mahatma Gandhi, Jawaharlal Nehru, and Subhas Chandra Bose, finished in India's statement of autonomy on August 15, 1947. The post-freedom time frame saw India wrestling with the intricacies of country building and the test of pro-ducing a cutting edge, industrialized country.

Jawaharlal Nehru, India's most memorable Head of the state, assumed a urgent part in molding the country's modern vision. His administration was set apart by the execution of the "Five-Year Plans," which expected to advance confidence and native modern turn of events. The plans laid the foundation for the development of key enterprises, including steel, coal, and power, and meant to decrease monetary reliance on far off nations.

One of the huge achievements in India's post-freedom industrialization was the Green Upheaval, started during the 1960s and 1970s. This groundbreaking development expected to increment rural efficiency through the reception of high-yielding harvest assortments, present day cultivating strategies, and better water system. The Green Upheaval prompted horticultural independence as well as made ready for the development of the food-handling industry, further differentiating the Indian economy.

The 1990s denoted a defining moment in India's modern scene with the progres-sion and globalization of the Indian economy. Under the initiative of then-State head P.V. Narasimha Rao and Money Priest Manmohan Singh, India set out on a way of financial changes. The destroying of the Permit Raj, which had smothered private endeavor, and the opening up of the economy to unfamiliar speculation were key to these changes. This period saw the rise of the data innovation (IT) and programming administrations area as a significant driver of India's monetary development.

The IT business, portrayed by organizations like Infosys, Wipro, and Goodbye Consultancy Administrations (TCS), utilized India's huge pool of gifted experts to turn into a worldwide IT center. By giving programming arrangements and administrations to clients around the world, India quickly earned respect as a mechanical force to be reckoned with and made a significant number of lucrative positions.

Notwithstanding the IT area, India's modern scene has broadened essentially. The country's drug industry, known for delivering reasonable conventional medications, has turned into a central part in the worldwide drug market. Indian car organizations, like Goodbye Engines and Mahindra and Mahindra, have secured themselves as both homegrown and global industry pioneers. These businesses have added to India's monetary development and advancement on the world stage.

In any case, India's modern process isn't without any trace of difficulties. The country wrestles with issues like administrative formality, administrative intricacies, and foundation bottlenecks that prevent the simplicity of carrying on with work. Land obtaining and work changes remain

subjects of extreme discussion. In addition, India's industrialization needs to resolve issues of monetary imbalance, territorial abberations, and ecological worries to guarantee that progress is both manageable and comprehensive.

1.2 Significance of India's Industrial Transformation

India's continuous modern change is a groundbreaking section in its set of experiences with significant ramifications for both the country and the worldwide local area. The meaning of this change reaches out a long ways past simple financial development; it addresses social, political, and natural viewpoints, introducing another time of potential outcomes and difficulties.

One of the most clear and significant components of India's modern change is monetary development. India's expanding modern area has been an impetus for the country's in general monetary development. As key ventures like data innovation, drugs, and assembling keep on flourishing, they contribute essentially to India's GDP (Gross domestic product) and create business open doors for a great many individuals. This financial development not just increases the expectation of living for some yet additionally reinforces India's situation in the worldwide monetary scene.

India's modern change likewise assumes a vital part in encouraging development and business. The nation's dynamic and lively beginning up environment has been earning overall respect. With a developing number of imaginative organizations and business visionaries entering the worldwide stage, India is cultivating a culture of development that reaches out past its lines. These pioneers are driving headways in innovation, science, and business, adding to India's scholarly capital and expanding its worldwide impact.

The modern area's extension has prompted the formation of a prospering working class, an essential power in India's financial and social scene. As additional individuals join the positions of the working class, buyer interest for labor and products keeps on rising, moving homegrown utilization. This expanded buying power benefits neighborhood organizations as well as draws in unfamiliar speculation and global partnerships, encouraging financial variety.

Moreover, India's modern change has impressive ramifications for business. The country's segment profit, portrayed by a youthful and developing populace, is saddled to fuel the modern labor force. India's modern development has made a huge number of open positions across different areas, giving work to millions and driving urbanization as individuals move to urban communities looking for better open doors. In any case, the test lies in guaranteeing that work creation stays up with the rising labor force, resolving issues of joblessness and underemployment.

The worldwide effect of India's modern change is additionally significant. As one of the world's most crowded countries, India's financial development has extensive ramifications. Its extending purchaser market offers critical open doors for global organizations looking to take advantage of its immense client base.

Furthermore, India's job in worldwide stock chains, especially in the data innovation and assembling areas, is turning out to be progressively basic. India's modern achievement has a gradually expanding influence, impacting exchange, venture, and global financial relations.

India's drug industry, specifically, plays had a significant impact in worldwide medical care. Known for its creation of reasonable nonexclusive medications, the nation has been instrumental in giving admittance to fundamental meds to individuals all over the planet. India's drug trades make medical services more available and reasonable for individuals in agricultural nations, adding to worldwide general wellbeing.

As India's modern change progresses, it additionally highlights the significance of economical turn of events. In a world confronting ecological difficulties, India's obligation to green advancements, sustainable power sources, and natural protection is critical. The nation is making progress in embracing clean energy arrangements, which decrease its carbon impression as well as add to worldwide endeavors to battle environmental change. As one of the world's biggest ozone depleting substance producers, India's progress to maintainable modern practices is indispensable for moderating the effects of environmental change.

The country's modern development likewise has critical ramifications for worldwide discretion and collaboration. India's development as a worldwide monetary power requires its dynamic cooperation in global associations, economic deals, and discussions. Its rising impact in these gatherings can possibly shape worldwide monetary approaches, exchange elements, and international procedures.

India's modern change isn't without its difficulties and intricacies. Issues like pay imbalance, territorial inconsistencies, and admittance to schooling and medical care should be addressed to guarantee that the advantages of modern development are comprehensive. Moreover, India faces the overwhelming errand of overseeing urbanization, framework improvement, and asset the executives while saving its social and regular legacy.

1.3 Objectives and Scope of the Book

This book intends to give an exhaustive investigation of India's modern ascent and its extraordinary excursion, revealing insight into the verifiable, financial, and social perspectives that have molded this noteworthy development. The essential goals and extent of this book can be summed up as follows:

Authentic Setting: The book will dive into India's verifiable setting, following the country's excursion from its antiquated civilization to pioneer oppression and post-freedom country building. Understanding the authentic underlying foundations of India's industrialization is fundamental to see the value in the difficulties and open doors that have denoted this change.

Financial Change: An inside and out assessment of the monetary parts of India's modern development will be a focal topic. This incorporates the advancement of key ventures, the job of business and development, and the effect on India's by and large financial scene.

Worldwide Ramifications: The book will investigate the worldwide ramifications of India's modern ascent, looking at what it means for global exchange, speculation, tact, and worldwide financial approaches. India's job in forming the world's financial future will be a focal concentration.

Social and Natural Aspects: The social and ecological outcomes of India's modern change will likewise be tended to. This incorporates looking at issues connected with pay imbalance, local inconsistencies, admittance to schooling and medical care, and India's endeavors to embrace supportable modern practices.

Difficulties and Amazing open doors: All through the book, the difficulties and valuable open doors that India faces in its modern process will be talked about. This incorporates issues, for example, administrative noise, administrative intricacies, framework bottlenecks, and the need to set out economical work open doors.

Comprehensive Development: A conspicuous topic of the book will be the accentuation on comprehensive development. It will feature the significance of guaranteeing that the advantages of modern development arrive at all sections of society and locales of the nation, resolving issues of financial imbalance and provincial abberations.

Supportable Turn of events: The book will accentuate the meaning of economical improvement in India's industrialization. It will investigate India's endeavors to take on clean energy arrangements, lessen its carbon impression, and add to worldwide drives to battle environmental change.

Worldwide Commitment: India's commitment to global associations, economic accords, and conciliatory relations will be examined to figure out the country's job on the worldwide stage and its effect on global arrangements and procedures.

Development and Business venture: The book will feature the developing society of advancement and business venture in India, especially with regards to the beginning up environment. It will talk about how these trailblazers are driving progressions in innovation and adding to India's scholarly capital.

Drug and IT Businesses: Unique consideration will be given to India's drug and data innovation enterprises, which play had a crucial impact in the country's modern development and worldwide impact. These enterprises are commendable examples of overcoming adversity that have had a tremendous effect around the world.

The extent of this book includes a great many points, from verifiable stories to contemporary financial examinations. It gives a multidisciplinary viewpoint that inspects India's modern change from different points. The book expects to take care of a different crowd, including understudies, researchers, policymakers, business pioneers, and anyone with any interest at all in acquiring a thorough comprehension of India's modern process.

Through the investigation of these targets and degree, this book looks to reveal insight into the multi-layered nature of India's modern change. It fills in as an important asset for those looking for bits of knowledge into the difficulties, valuable open doors, and meaning of India's modern ascent in the worldwide setting.

Chapter 2

Early Foundations

The excursion of life starts with the fragile, yet getting through embroidered artwork of our earliest establishments. These early stages shape us, form our personality, and impact our future. It is during this period that we move into the obscure, both in a real sense and figuratively, as we explore the mind boggling trap of human turn of events.

From the snapshot of our introduction to the world, we are pushed into a universe of tactile over-burden. The delicate dash of a mother's hand, the calming cradlesongs that serenade our fantasies, and the fragrance of home are our underlying anchors. These tactile encounters lay the basis for how we might interpret the world and our place inside it. As we develop, our faculties grow, and we start to investigate the limits of our reality. We handle at vivid toys, taste new flavors, and pay attention to the orchestra of life unfurling around us.

Quite possibly of the most significant and getting through relationship we structure during these early years is with our parental figures. Whether it's our folks, grandparents, or different watchmen, they assume a basic part in supporting and directing us. Their adoration and care give the profound establishment whereupon we assemble our identity worth, security, and confidence on the planet. These early bonds set up for our future connections, affecting our capacity to associate with others and to communicate our feelings.

Language arises as an incredible asset during this time. As newborn children, we murmur and coo, bit by bit advancing into prattling and, in the end, lucid discourse. The obtaining of language is a surprising accomplishment that permits us to convey, share our necessities and wants, and figure out the considerations and sensations of people around us. Through the words we hear and the words we express, we start to figure out the world and our place in it. Language turns into the scaffold that interfaces us to the immense domain of human information and culture.

In these early years, our minds are like wipes, absorbing information at an astounding rate. We learn through play, investigation, and perception. Our general surroundings turns into a study hall, and each experience is an example. We find the enchantment of circumstances and logical results, the delight of disclosure, and the excitement of achievement. Our mental advancement makes its most memorable strides, establishing the groundwork for future learning and critical thinking.

Creative mind blossoms in this fruitful soil of youth. Kids make striking universes to them, populated by fantastical animals and trying undertakings. Through play, they foster fundamental mental and interactive abilities.

Pretending shows them sympathy and the specialty of participation, while working with blocks or drawing pictures practices fine coordinated abilities and inventiveness. Creative mind, joined with the boundless interest of youth, drives the hunger for information and investigation.

As we develop, our bodies and brains go through quick changes. We foster the coordinated abilities important to creep, walk, and at last run. This freshly discovered portability opens up a universe of potential outcomes, as we investigate the limits of our actual capacities. We figure out how to take care of ourselves, dress, and care for our own requirements. The developing autonomy is both exciting and testing, as we find the results of our activities and the requirement for obligation.

Early training is a basic component in our formative process. Preschools, kindergartens, and youth programs give organized conditions where kids can learn, mingle, and plan for the proper schooling that lies ahead. Here, they create the primary abilities of perusing, composing, and math, fabricating the system for a long period of learning. Early training additionally underscores socialization, assisting youngsters with communicating with peers, resolve clashes, and grasp the upsides of participation and regard.

The family climate assumes a critical part in molding our qualities, convictions, and social personality. Our families acquaint us with the traditions, customs, and ceremonies that structure the bedrock of our social legacy. These early openings are instrumental in molding our feeling of having a place, assisting us with embracing variety, and encouraging an appreciation for the rich embroidery of human culture.

In these basic years, our close to home improvement becomes the overwhelming focus. We experience a scope of feelings, from delight and miracle to dissatisfaction and trouble. These close to home encounters are essential for figuring out how to manage our sentiments and explore the intricacies of human connections. As we experience disillusionment and difficulty, we start to foster strength, figuring out how to return from mishaps and face life's difficulties sincerely and mental fortitude.

Youth additionally denotes the start of our moral and moral turn of events. We begin to recognize right from off-base, directed by the ethical compass of our parental figures and social qualities. These early examples lay the preparation for our feeling of equity, sympathy, and moral direction. We discover that activities have results and that our decisions influence people around us.

The universe of stories and books opens up new skylines during these early years. Sleep time stories, tales, and picture books become windows to different universes, lighting our minds and extending how we might interpret language. The adoration for perusing is sustained in these early days, making ready for a deep rooted relationship with the composed word. Narrating turns into an extension to sympathy, permitting us to step into the shoes of characters and experience their feelings and undertakings.

The significance of actual wellbeing is highlighted during youth. Legitimate sustenance, exercise, and customary clinical check-ups are crucial for help the developing body. These propensities establish the groundwork for a sound way of life that can reach out all through our lives. Early openness to sports and pro-active tasks cultivates an adoration for development and rivalry, empowering the improvement of actual wellness and coordination.

Artistic expressions assume an imperative part in youth improvement, starting imagination and self-articulation. Through drawing, painting, moving, and music, kids figure out how to impart their feelings and thoughts in non-verbal ways. Creative undertakings additionally improve fine coordinated abilities and give a road to investigating their inward universes.

Early establishments stretch out past the home and school, including the more extensive local area and society. In these early stages, youngsters start to accept the idea of citizenship and their part on the planet. They notice the activities and ways of behaving of grown-ups and begin to shape their own viewpoints about cultural standards and values. Local area commitment and chipping in exercises can additionally impart a feeling of obligation and compassion for other people.

2.1 From Agrarian Society to Early Industries

The change of human social orders from agrarian-based economies to early industrialization denoted a urgent defining moment ever, reshaping the manner in which individuals lived, worked, and communicated with their general surroundings. This progress, crossing from the late eighteenth to the mid nineteenth hundreds of years, had expansive outcomes, setting off significant changes in innovation, culture, and the construction of society.

Agrarian culture, which had ruled for quite a long time, was described by a principally rustic populace participated in farming. Most of individuals resided in little, self-supporting networks, where life spun around the development of harvests and the raising of animals. The land was the wellspring of riches and influence, with primitive frameworks frequently characterizing connections between land-owners, workers, and workers. Advancements in agribusiness, like the reception of yield pivot and worked on cultivating procedures, had been consistently expanding food creation. Be that as it may, as populaces developed, the constraints of agrarian culture became clear, and the requirement for change arose.

The impetus for this change was the Modern Upheaval. It started in England and afterward spread to different pieces of Europe and the US, on a very basic level modifying how work was coordinated and the method for creation. The mechanical developments that drove the Modern Upheaval, similar to the steam motor, automated material creation, and further developed transportation, upset businesses. Processing plants and factories supplanted customary bungalow ventures, and large scale manufacturing turned into the standard. This shift from a generally agrarian economy to one progressively dependent on industry had significant ramifications.

Urbanization was one of the most noticeable indications of this change. As industrialization picked up speed, individuals rushed to urban areas looking for business. The once calm, agrarian towns expanded into clamoring cities. The cadence of life changed, as the peaceful field gave approach to the swarmed, boisterous, and frequently unsanitary states of the modern urban communities. The relocation of individuals from country to metropolitan regions flagged a shift in monetary open doors as well as in social and social elements. Metropolitan life presented new difficulties and valuable open doors, and the quick development of urban communities required huge changes in foundation and administration.

The plant framework, a sign of the Modern Insurgency, upset work and creation. It denoted a shift from individual craftsmans and craftspeople to huge scope fabricating. Laborers presently toiled in processing plants, where machines were the focal method for creation. The division of work turned out to be progressively particular, with people performing monotonous assignments. This prompted more prominent productivity yet in addition made repetitive, frequently dehumanizing, workplaces. Worker's guilds and laborers' developments arose because of these circumstances, looking to work on working circumstances, compensation, and the freedoms of laborers.

Mechanical advancement was at the core of the Modern Upheaval. The creation of the steam motor, credited to James Watt, was a distinct advantage. It controlled machines as well as changed transportation, prompting the improvement of steam trains and steamships, which worked with the development of products and individuals on an extraordinary scale. The material business was another field where development proliferated. The turning jenny, power loom, and cotton gin changed the development of materials, making them more open and reasonable. The improvement of the message and the railroad additionally worked with correspondence and transportation, making a trap of network that reached out across mainlands.

Developments in assembling and transportation were combined with the development of worldwide exchange. The Modern Upheaval changed homegrown economies as well as significantly affected the worldwide stage. The extension of business sectors and the expanded trade of merchandise and thoughts reshaped the worldwide scene. European powers vied for provinces in Africa, Asia, and the Americas to get assets and new business sectors for their modern items. This drive for government had significant results on the social orders and societies of colonized districts, adding to the spread of Western impact and values.

The effect of the Modern Upheaval reached out past financial matters and innovation; it was profoundly interwoven with culture and society. The ascent of modern free enterprise and the fast speed of progress encouraged new qualities and philosophies. Social ordered progressions started to move, and the customary jobs of family and local area advanced. The rise of a working class, enabled by financial open doors and schooling, reshaped social designs and tested laid out standards.

The Illumination, which had laid the scholarly preparation for political and social change, tracked down fruitful ground amidst industrialization. Thoughts of individual freedoms, a majority rules government, and secularism built up some decent forward momentum, prompting political insurgencies and change developments. The French Transformation, with its call for freedom, fairness, and brotherhood, shook the groundworks of government and nobility. These thoughts likewise impacted the arrangement of current country states and the drafting of constitutions.

The impacts of industrialization were not uniform across social orders. While it carried thriving to some, it additionally exacerbated social disparities and work abuse. Youngster work, long working hours, and unfortunate working circumstances were uncontrolled in numerous enterprises, prompting calls for change and guideline. The work development acquired strength, supporting for laborers' freedoms and pushing for regulations to further develop conditions.

The job of ladies in the public eye additionally went through massive change. As plant work turned out to be more normal, ladies entered the labor force in more noteworthy numbers, testing conventional orientation jobs. While open doors opened up for some, numerous ladies actually confronted segregation and restricted admittance to schooling and administrative roles.

The shift from agrarian culture to early enterprises was not without its difficulties and intricacies. It denoted a time of dynamic change, with both positive and unfortunate results. Financial development and innovative advancement brought success and worked on expectations for everyday comforts for the vast majority, yet they likewise made new types of disparity and social issues. The Modern Unrest significantly affected all parts of life - from where and how individuals resided to how they functioned and collaborated with the world. As it unfurled, it put into high gear a direction that would keep on molding the cutting edge world for a long time into the future.

2.2 Cottage Industries and Traditional Craftsmanship

In the midst of the flood of industrialization during the eighteenth and nineteenth hundreds of years, an equal universe of craftsmanship and cabin businesses endured, commending the masterfulness and commitment of gifted people who handmade merchandise. These conventional practices were well established in neighborhood networks and assumed an imperative part in saving social legacy, while giving an offset to the motorized, large scale manufacturing of the Modern Unrest.

House businesses, described by limited scope, locally established creation, were a foundation of pre-modern economies. Gifted craftsmans and craftspeople worked from their homes or little studios, making a wide cluster of handcrafted items, from materials and earthenware to metalwork and carpentry. This decentralized model of creation took into consideration a private association between the maker and the customer. It likewise encouraged a feeling of local area, as neighbors frequently met up to participate in cooperative work, sharing information and strategies went down through ages.

Conventional craftsmanship thrived across the world, creating things prestigious for their excellence, quality, and social importance. For example, in India, unpredictable handwoven materials like silk and cotton sarees were carefully created by talented craftsmans, every area having its own unmistakable procedures and plans. Also, in Japan, the specialty of earthenware, as exemplified by wonderful porcelain and pottery from locales like Arita and Kyoto, was worshipped for its tasteful and practical characteristics. Customary craftsmanship was an impression of the nearby culture and customs, frequently integrating native materials and strategies, making every item a one of a kind masterpiece.

The safeguarding of conventional craftsmanship was profoundly interlaced with social personality. In numerous social orders, distinctive abilities were gone down through ages, with information and procedures protected as a piece of the social legacy. The student framework was basic to this interaction, as hopeful craftsmans gained from aces, copying their strategies and masterfulness. This mentorship guaranteed the congruity of craftsmanship while supporting a deep satisfaction and reason inside the local area.

The tasteful magnificence of conventional craftsmanship was frequently indivisible from its usefulness. High quality items, whether stoneware, materials, or metalwork, bore the sign of individual innovativeness and craftsmanship. These items filled commonsense needs, yet they rose above the utilitarian by mirroring the imaginative sensibilities of their makers. This combination of workmanship and utility was a sign of conventional craftsmanship, enhancing daily existence with objects that were practical as well as gorgeous.

Bungalow ventures and customary craftsmanship likewise embraced maintainability some time before it turned into a popular expression. These craftsmans were frequently profoundly associated with the materials they utilized, obtaining them locally and utilizing eco-accommodating procedures. The act of upcycling and reusing materials was typical, as waste was limited, and assets were used to their fullest degree. The emphasis on making strong, great merchandise was a major precept of customary craftsmanship, remaining as a conspicuous difference to the expendable culture that arose with industrialization.

Besides, conventional craftsmanship assumed a crucial part in saving the abilities and strategies that were fundamental for some social orders' independence. In provincial and agrarian economies, the capacity to make apparel, apparatuses, and family things was fundamental for endurance. The information on these abilities was gone down through ages, guaranteeing that networks could support themselves and keep a level of freedom.

Customary craftsmanship was not without its difficulties. The time and expertise expected for handcrafting restricted the size of creation, making hand tailored merchandise more costly and less open to the more extensive populace. As the Modern Transformation picked up speed, efficiently manufactured, machine-made items turned out to be more reasonable and promptly accessible, representing an imposing test to the conventional craftsmans.

Bungalow businesses, while treasured, confronted monetary tensions that frequently prompted their downfall.

In any case, the appreciation for customary craftsmanship never vanished altogether. Indeed, even as motorization and industrialization reshaped economies and social orders, there stayed a specialty market for hand tailored, high quality items. This was driven by a longing for credibility and a dismissal of the homogenization that accompanied efficiently manufactured merchandise. Customers searched out carefully assembled things, esteeming the narratives, culture, and masterfulness that accompanied them. Craftsmanship, in numerous ways, encountered a resurgence in the late twentieth and mid 21st hundreds of years, as a counter-development against the unoriginal idea of modern items.

The rejuvenation of customary craftsmanship was worked with by the world-wide market's capacity to associate craftsmans with purchasers from everywhere the world. Web based business stages, craftsman markets, and fair exchange drives permitted conventional specialties to track down a more extensive crowd, giving a type of revenue to gifted craftsmans and a stage to grandstand their gifts. Along these lines, customary craftsmanship adjusted to the computerized age, tracking down a space close by large scale manufacturing, and profiting from the acknowledgment of its innate worth.

2.3 Role of Cottage Industries in Laying the Foundation

Cabin ventures play had a critical impact in forming the monetary and social scene of various social orders, particularly during the beginning stages of industrialization. They filled in as the primary stones whereupon current economies were fabricated, contributing essentially to monetary development, business age, and local area advancement.

Cabin enterprises, portrayed by limited scope, decentralized creation, frequently worked inside the bounds of individual homes or little studios. These undertakings traversed different areas, including materials, crafted works, agro-handling, from there, the sky is the limit. The meaning of house businesses lay in their capacity to give a method for occupation to neighborhood networks, especially in country regions.

One of the most major commitments of cabin businesses was their part in work age. In pre-modern social orders, where farming work was occasional and unusual, cabin ventures offered a consistent type of revenue for rustic populaces. Gifted craftsmans, frequently with profound roots in their networks, were the foundation of these ventures, utilizing conventional strategies and information went down through ages. In that capacity, they gave business open doors as well as protected social legacy and craftsmanship.

House businesses additionally enabled ladies in numerous social orders. These businesses permitted ladies to work from the bounds of their homes, making it simpler to offset family obligations with monetary exercises. This was particularly huge in social orders where ladies' jobs were generally restricted to homegrown tasks.

Cabin enterprises furnished ladies with chances to add to their family's pay, consequently upgrading their monetary freedom and social standing.

The creation processes inside cabin ventures were frequently profoundly work escalated, including perplexing manual work. This supported nearby work as well as guaranteed that networks remained intently weave. The cooperative idea of cabin enterprises implied that individuals frequently cooperated, sharing information and abilities inside the local area. These common exercises encouraged a feeling of fellowship and local area, which was fundamental for social union.

The results of cabin enterprises were famous for their quality and uniqueness. Handmade things bore the unmistakable bit of their creators, mirroring their imaginative sensibilities and nearby social subtleties. This individualized way to deal with creation made areas of strength for a between the craftsman and the buyer, frequently bringing about a reliable client base. The worth of high quality items rose above simple utility; they were permeated with the narratives, culture, and legacy of their makers.

Besides, cabin businesses were instrumental in advancing supportability. A significant number of these ventures depended on privately obtained unrefined components, lessening the ecological impression related with transportation and large scale manufacturing. Moreover, conventional strategies frequently focused on asset effectiveness, as craftsmans were enthusiastic about limiting waste and augmenting the utilization of accessible materials. These practices lined up with reasonable standards, well before supportability turned into a standard concern.

Bungalow ventures were not without their difficulties. They frequently confronted restrictions as far as scale, which made it challenging for them to rival enormous scope modern creation regarding amount and cost. The appearance of industrialization and motorization introduced imposing difficulties to the cabin business model, as efficiently manufactured merchandise overflowed the market, offering less expensive other options.

Regardless, house ventures figured out how to persevere, adjusting to changing times and utilizing their innate benefits. Now and again, they tracked down new business sectors and customers that valued the worth of hand tailored, distinctive items. The computerized age and the ascent of internet business stages gave a worldwide stage to cabin enterprises to grandstand their items and interface with shoppers from everywhere the world. These computerized stages permitted craftsmans to extend their range while holding their unmistakable way to deal with creation.

Early establishments are basic to grasping the turn of events and progress of human civilization. These developmental phases of history set up for the rise of complicated social orders, mechanical progressions, and social advancement.

In this investigation of early establishments, we will dig into the beginnings of human progress, the development of horticulture, the ascent of antiquated realms, and the advancement of key social and mechanical accomplishments that laid the preparation for the cutting edge world.

The starting points of human progress can be followed back to the change from hunting and assembling to settled agribusiness. This stupendous shift, known as the Neolithic Insurgency, happened roughly quite a while back. Before this change, early people carried on with traveling lives, hunting and rummaging for food. The improvement of farming denoted a huge defining moment, empowering individuals to develop crops and train animals, which gave a more steady and solid food source.

Agribusiness permitted people to get comfortable one spot, prompting the foundation of super durable towns and networks. The capacity to store overflow food set out open doors for specialization, as certain people could zero in on errands other than food creation. This specialization led to a division of work, where individuals created skill in different exchanges and specialties, like ceramics, toolmaking, and development. Accordingly, the early underpinnings of perplexing social orders started to arise.

The development of settled networks and the overflow of food achieved another essential turn of events - the ascent of progress. The absolute earliest realized developments can be tracked down in Mesopotamia (cutting edge Iraq), Egypt, the Indus Valley (advanced Pakistan and northwest India), and China. These old civilizations shared normal qualities, like unified administration, coordinated farming, and composed language.

In Mesopotamia, the Sumerians created one of the world's earliest composing frameworks known as cuneiform, which was recorded on earth tablets. This development worked with record-keeping as well as considered the scattering of information and the protection of social and authentic data. Essentially, in Egypt, hieroglyphics were utilized to record strict and managerial data on papyrus. The capacity to record and communicate information turned into a foundation of early civilizations and a fundamental starting point for future scholarly and social headways.

The ascent of progress likewise prompted the development of unified legislatures, frequently as city-states or realms. These early political elements executed frameworks of regulations, tax collection, and organization. In Mesopotamia, for instance, the Code of Hammurabi, one of the world's most established legitimate codes, gave rules to equity and administration. Such frameworks of administration kept everything under control and soundness, which were fundamental for the development and supportability of early social orders.

The advancement of coordinated religion was one more essential part of early establishments. Strict convictions and practices were profoundly entwined with the day to day routines of old individuals. In Mesopotamia, the Sumerians loved a pantheon of divine beings, and sanctuaries were built as focuses of strict and social action.

Likewise, in antiquated Egypt, the development of amazing pyramids and sanctuaries, as well as the preservation of the departed, mirrored the meaning of strict convictions in the public arena.

Social accomplishments in early developments stretched out past religion and administration. The development of structural marvels, like the ziggurats of Mesopotamia, the pyramids of Egypt, and the extraordinary walls of China, exhibited progressed designing and engineering abilities. These fantastic designs not just displayed the may and resourcefulness of these social orders yet in addition filled pragmatic needs, including guard and flood control.

The improvement of composing, math, and science stamped critical steps in human comprehension and scholarly advancement. Early numerical frameworks, for example, the cuneiform-based arithmetic of the Babylonians, laid the foundation for the further developed numerical ideas we use today. Also, headways in medication and space science were made in antiquated Mesopotamia. The antiquated Greeks, expanding upon the information on their ancestors, made striking commitments to reasoning, science, and arithmetic, establishing the groundworks for Western scholarly customs.

Exchange assumed an essential part interfacing early civic establishments, working with the trading of merchandise, thoughts, and culture. The Silk Street, for instance, associated the East and West, considering the exchange of silk, flavors, and other important products. The interconnectedness of these areas added to the dissemination of innovations, ways of thinking, and religions, advancing the embroidered artwork of human development.

The early underpinnings of human civilization additionally saw the advancement of legitimate and philosophical thoughts that keep on impacting current cultures. In antiquated Greece, the scholars Plato and Aristotle made critical commitments to moral and political idea. Their thoughts regarding equity, a majority rules system, and administration keep on being examined and bantered in the contemporary world.

The lawful customs of antiquated human advancements have likewise left enduring heritages. The Roman Republic, trailed by the Roman Realm, fostered a refined general set of laws, which incorporated the well known "Twelve Tables" of Roman regulation. Roman regulation filled in as a model for the vast majority general sets of laws that observed, remembering current common regulation frameworks for Europe and Latin America.

Strict convictions and practices that began in the early underpinnings of human advancement keep on forming societies and social orders all over the planet. The strict customs of old Mesopotamia, Egypt, India, and China significantly affect the improvement of strict idea and practice. A considerable lot of the moral and moral standards enunciated in these early strict texts are still basic for contemporary strict and philosophical convictions.

The early underpinnings of progress were likewise set apart by times of extension and struggle. The tactical missions and regional victories of old realms, like the Persian Domain, the Roman Realm, and the Maurya Domain, brought various districts and people groups under unified rule. These domains presented frameworks of administration, foundation, and exchange that significantly affected the social orders they dominated.

The old Roman Realm, for instance, laid out a huge organization of streets, reservoir conduits, and legitimate establishments that impacted later European developments. The spread of Roman regulation, specifically, assumed a critical part in the improvement of current general sets of laws. Also, the Silk Street and the sea shipping lanes of the Indian Sea associated far off lands and worked with the trading of products, thoughts, and societies.

The fall of old domains frequently stamped times of progress and change. As domains declined, new social orders and societies arose. This peculiarity was clear in the fall of the Western Roman Domain, which brought about the archaic period in Europe. The breakdown of the Roman Realm prompted the discontinuity of political power and the decentralization of force. Medieval frameworks, where nearby rulers controlled land and assets, became predominant, and another social order arose.

During the archaic period, the underpinnings of present day Europe came to fruition. The Catholic Church assumed a focal part in middle age society, serving as a strict establishment as well as a political and social power. The advancement of feudalism, with its perplexing arrangement of commitments and land possession, formed the construction of archaic culture.

Innovative and scholarly progressions during the archaic period laid the basis for the Renaissance and the inevitable development of the advanced world. Developments in farming, like the weighty furrow and the three-field framework, further developed food creation and added to populace development. Also, the foundation of colleges in middle age Europe gave focuses to learning and the trading of information, which added to logical, philosophical, and imaginative advancement.

The Renaissance, which started in Italy in the fourteenth hundred years, denoted a time of recharged interest in traditional workmanship, culture, and information. Crafted by specialists like Leonardo da Vinci, Michelangelo, and Raphael, as well as the works of masterminds like Galileo and Copernicus, exemplified the scholarly and imaginative accomplishments of this period.

Bungalow businesses play had a fundamental impact in molding the monetary and social scene of different social orders over the entire course of time. These limited scale, decentralized types of creation include the making of products inside individual families or little studios, frequently utilizing customary and manual procedures. The job of cabin ventures in establishing the groundwork for bigger, modern economies is diverse, as they have added to monetary turn of events, business, and social conservation.

Cabin ventures are well established throughout the entire existence of human civilizations. Before the appearance of huge scope industrialization, most creation happened inside families or little, limited studios. Individuals created merchandise like materials, ceramics, devices, and horticultural items utilizing difficult work and basic instruments. These bungalow ventures were fundamental for meeting the essential necessities of people and networks.

In numerous areas, the advancement of cabin businesses was intently attached to the accessibility of neighborhood assets and customary craftsmanship. For instance, districts with bountiful fleece assets frequently saw the ascent of bungalow ventures zeroed in on turning, winding around, and delivering materials. Nearby craftsmans and craftspeople utilized their skill to make great merchandise that were sought after inside their networks and then some.

The financial meaning of bungalow enterprises couldn't possibly be more significant. They frequently gave jobs to a significant piece of the populace, particularly in agrarian social orders. By and large, bungalow ventures were entwined with agrarian cycles, as ranchers and rustic families took part in material creation, earthenware making, or different specialties during horticultural slow times of year. This beneficial pay helped cradle families against the dangers related with cultivating.

Bungalow businesses additionally offered adaptability and versatility, empowering people to offset their jobs with different obligations. For instance, ladies oftentimes participated in bungalow businesses like winding around and turning, permitting them to add to their families' pay while overseeing homegrown obligations.

The effect of bungalow businesses reached out past individual families. The deal and trade of products created by these ventures frequently framed the premise of neighborhood and provincial exchange organizations. Towns and towns became focuses of creation and exchange, making monetary interdependencies and reinforcing local area bonds.

House ventures assumed an essential part in protecting and sending social legacy. Customary craftsmanship was gone down through ages, with families or neighborhood societies keeping up with and refining their methods. The creation of carefully assembled merchandise, whether materials, pottery, or carpentry, frequently bore remarkable territorial qualities and plans that reflected nearby culture and character.

These enterprises additionally added to the advancement of high quality abilities and mastery. Craftsmans and craftspeople sharpened their procedures over the long run, dominating the complexities of their specialties. Apprenticeships and casual learning were normal, guaranteeing the progression of information and ability move across ages. The conservation of these conventional abilities stays a fundamental part of cabin enterprises today.

The coming of enormous scope industrialization, especially during the eighteenth and nineteenth hundreds of years, carried massive changes to the monetary scene. Modern processing plants, automation, and large scale manufacturing arose, supplanting or changing numerous bungalow businesses. While the shift to enormous scope modern creation was driven by innovative progressions and the quest for more prominent effectiveness, it additionally introduced new open doors and difficulties.

The progress from house ventures to huge scope industrialization made a few significant impacts. From one perspective, it expanded the creation limit and result of products, which added to monetary development and the ascent of buyer culture. Efficiently manufactured things turned out to be more reasonable and open, prompting enhancements in expectations for everyday comforts for some.

Then again, the shift to industrialization additionally introduced difficulties. Industrial facility work frequently expected workers to pass on their homes and move to metropolitan focuses, upsetting laid out examples of life and local area. The division of work in processing plants decreased laborers' jobs to explicit, dull undertakings, rather than the different and diverse jobs they frequently played in bungalow enterprises. Work conditions in plants were at times cruel, and worries about laborers' freedoms and prosperity arose.

Nonetheless, bungalow businesses didn't vanish with the ascent of industrialization. In many areas of the planet, limited scope, locally situated creation continued and, surprisingly, adjusted to the new modern scene. House businesses kept on flourishing in locales where motorized industrialization had not yet completely grabbed hold, or where there was an interest for top caliber, hand tailored merchandise.

As a matter of fact, human expression and specialties development that arose in the late nineteenth and mid twentieth hundreds of years was a response to the apparent dehumanization of work in modern manufacturing plants. Promoters of this development supported the safeguarding of customary craftsmanship and the formation of carefully assembled, high quality products. This development assumed a part in reviving bungalow businesses and advancing the worth of hand-crafted items.

Besides, house enterprises have kept on advancing in light of changing monetary and mechanical scenes. The appearance of the web and internet business stages has empowered craftsmans and craftspeople to contact a worldwide crowd, interfacing with purchasers who value the uniqueness and independence of handmade things. Numerous craftsmans have utilized web-based commercial centers to sell their products, permitting bungalow businesses to thrive in the computerized age.

Moreover, house enterprises are progressively perceived for their capability to drive maintainable and harmless to the ecosystem creation. The utilization of normal, privately obtained materials and the shortfall of enormous scope apparatus can lessen the carbon impression of bungalow enterprises. As manageability turns into a focal worry in contemporary society, the resurgence of house enterprises lines up with the developing interest for eco-accommodating, hand tailored items.

Cabin ventures are not restricted to customary specialties like materials or ceramics; they incorporate many exercises, including food creation, high quality refreshments, and carefully assembled cleansers. In the food business, limited scope ranchers and makers of specialty products have embraced the standards of bungalow enterprises. They focus on quality, neighborhood fixings, and customary techniques to make exceptional, top notch items.

One of the vital qualities of bungalow ventures lies in their capacity to answer market patterns and purchaser inclinations quickly. These businesses frequently produce little clumps of merchandise, which can be adjusted and altered to fulfill changing shopper needs. For instance, the specialty lager industry has seen exceptional development, driven by shoppers looking for unmistakable, privately blended drinks. Little specialty breweries can try different things with different fixings and preparing strategies to make exceptional flavors and styles, taking care of assorted preferences.

Bungalow businesses are likewise pivotal in cultivating business venture and supporting nearby economies. Limited scope, high quality creation frequently gives open doors to people to begin their own organizations and be independently employed. Business visionaries can transform their enthusiasm and abilities into a kind of revenue, adding to neighborhood monetary turn of events and setting out work open doors inside their networks.

Moreover, the renaissance of bungalow businesses has acquired consideration as a way to revive country regions and protect conventional societies. Numerous rustic networks have encountered termination and monetary decay, as more youthful ages relocate to metropolitan focuses looking for work amazing open doors. House enterprises can offer another option, permitting individuals to work and flourish while staying in the places where they grew up.

The resurgence of house enterprises lines up with a more extensive cultural shift toward manageability, privately obtained items, and an emphasis on higher expectations when in doubt. Shoppers progressively look for items with a straightforward store network, an association with the maker, and an accentuation on natural obligation. These qualities reverberate with the standards of cabin businesses, which frequently focus on moral creation, decrease waste, and backing neighborhood networks.

Chapter 3

The Birth of Large-Scale Industry

The introduction of huge scope industry in the late eighteenth and mid nineteenth hundreds of years denoted a groundbreaking crossroads in mankind's set of experiences. It introduced another time of mechanical development, financial extension, and cultural change, on a very basic level modifying the manner in which individuals worked, lived, and cooperated with the world. This fantastic shift was energized by a conversion of variables, remembering progresses for innovation, changes underway techniques, and the ascent of free enterprise.

One of the critical drivers behind the introduction of enormous scope industry was the advancement of new innovations. The steam motor, spearheaded by James Watt, was a weighty creation that reformed the method for creation. It gave a wellspring of mechanical power that could drive hardware, empowering manufacturing plants to motorize creation processes that were once work concentrated and dependent on human or creature muscle. The steam motor's capacity to create energy from the burning of coal or different energizes was a distinct advantage, giving a predictable and strong wellspring of force that could be tackled for a great many modern applications.

This mechanical jump was supplemented by advancements in hardware. The material business, one of the first to embrace motorization, saw the appearance of machines like the turning jenny and the power loom. These gadgets essentially expanded the proficiency and speed of material creation, making it conceivable to make textures on a scale that had been unfathomable with difficult work alone. Different ventures immediately took action accordingly, automating their cycles and accomplishing levels of efficiency that were already incomprehensible.

The reception of new creation techniques was likewise a basic component in the introduction of enormous scope industry. Before this time, creation was in many cases coordinated around little, bungalow enterprises, where gifted craftsmans or laborers delivered products on a more limited size, habitually in their homes or little studios. These decentralized creation strategies were portrayed by a serious level of craftsmanship yet restricted yield. Be that as it may, the Modern Transformation presented the plant framework, which incorporated creation and increased it altogether. Plants became center points of large scale manufacturing, lodging hardware, and a developing labor force. This brought together methodology empowered economies of scale and a significant expansion in the amount of merchandise created.

The development of enormous scope industry was naturally connected to the ascent of free enterprise. Free enterprise, as a financial and social framework, focuses on confidential responsibility for method for creation and the quest for benefit.

This way of thinking gave the vital structure to the development of huge scope industry, as business visionaries and industrialists looked to gain by new innovations and creation techniques to build their riches. The benefit rationale filled in as a strong impetus for development and interest in enormous scope industry.

The introduction of huge scope industry prompted significant changes in the manner individuals worked. With the change from house ventures to production lines, the workforce encountered a huge shift. Laborers, when independently employed or took part in limited scope high quality creation, presently ended up as pay workers in enormous plants. The industrial facility framework presented another division of work, with laborers doled out unambiguous, frequently redundant undertakings on the sequential construction system. While these positions were in some cases repetitive and requesting, they gave a level of employer stability and a standard pay for a developing metropolitan labor force.

Urbanization was one more outcome of the introduction of enormous scope industry. As production lines and modern focuses extended, country populaces ran to urban communities looking for work open doors. The once prevalently agrarian scene of numerous social orders was quickly changed into a clamoring organization of modern towns and urban communities. The development of metropolitan regions achieved huge changes in everyday environments, framework, and social elements.

The circumstances in early modern production lines were frequently difficult and, now and again, unforgiving. Long working hours, low wages, and unfortunate working circumstances were normal. The wellbeing and security of laborers were every now and again neglected, and trade guilds and laborers' developments arose in light of these circumstances, pushing for further developed work environment conditions, fair wages, and laborers' privileges.

The introduction of enormous scope industry likewise had extensive consequences for society and culture. The large scale manufacturing of merchandise, worked with by motorization and centralization of creation, brought about the accessibility of a wide cluster of items to a more extensive crowd. The shopper culture started to come to fruition, as people approached a more extensive scope of merchandise, changing their ways of life and utilization propensities.

Moreover, the extension of the production line framework and the ascent of huge scope industry had critical international results. The requirement for unrefined substances to take care of the always developing apparatus and the quest for new business sectors for modern items prompted the imperialistic extension of European powers into states in Africa, Asia, and the Americas. This scramble for assets and markets significantly affected the colonized areas, influencing their societies, economies, and social orders.

The introduction of enormous scope industry likewise lastingly affected the indigenous habitat. The expanded utilization of coal and other petroleum derivatives to drive the modern machines prompted more significant levels of air contamination and added to the development of ecological worries.

The development of industry prepared for the advancement of the cutting edge ecological development as individuals perceived the outcomes of industrialization in the world.

3.1 Emergence of Early Factories

The development of early processing plants during the Modern Transformation in the late eighteenth and mid nineteenth hundreds of years denoted a significant change in the manner merchandise were created. It laid the preparation for present day modern free enterprise and presented another time of automation, centralization, and large scale manufacturing. The industrial facility framework, a sign of this change, upset the universe of work, fundamentally influencing the economy, society, and culture.

Industrial facilities addressed a crucial takeoff from customary creation strategies. Before their rise, creation was principally decentralized, with gifted craftsmans and little studios making products on a limited scale. These limited scale tasks were many times work escalated, depending on craftsmanship, and were restricted in their result. Be that as it may, the manufacturing plant framework packed creation in a solitary, unified area, uniting hardware, unrefined components, and a developing workforce under one rooftop. This centralization considered the use of huge scope automation and the coordination of different creation processes.

The motorization of creation was a characterizing component of early plants. The accessibility of steam motors and different wellsprings of mechanical power permitted machines to assume control over errands that were recently performed by human or creature work. For instance, material industrial facilities used turning jennies, power lingers, and checking machines to mechanize the development of materials, altogether expanding result and productivity. This motorization achieved a change in outlook underway strategies, changing numerous businesses and establishing the groundwork for present day fabricating.

The division of work was one more vital component of the manufacturing plant framework. This approach involved separating complex creation processes into more modest, specific undertakings that singular laborers could perform. Laborers were not generally expected to be flexible craftsmans; all things considered, they were relegated explicit, frequently redundant, errands on the sequential construction system. This division of work empowered plants to accomplish more prominent effectiveness, as every specialist could zero in on a solitary part of creation. The sequential construction system, with its specialization and effectiveness, turned into a sign of early plants and a model that would be copied across different ventures.

The manufacturing plant framework in a general sense changed the idea of work. Dissimilar to the decentralized, frequently independently employed craftsmans of the past, laborers in production lines were currently wage workers. They offered their work to plant proprietors and were in many cases subject to fixed working hours and production line discipline. While the plant framework brought a level of employer stability and a standard pay, it likewise presented another arrangement of difficulties for laborers.

Long working hours, low wages, and in some cases cruel working circumstances were normal, prompting work developments and the support for further developed work environment conditions and laborers' freedoms.

Urbanization was an immediate result of the rise of production lines. As modern focuses extended, country populaces ran to urban areas looking for work valuable open doors. The development of metropolitan regions was fast and emotional, changing the dominatingly agrarian scenes of numerous social orders into clamoring modern towns and urban areas. Urbanization altogether affected everyday environments, framework, and social elements. It prompted the advancement of new types of lodging, transportation organizations, and public administrations to oblige the developing metropolitan populace.

Early industrial facilities were focuses of creation as well as strong specialists of social and social change. The centralization of individuals in manufacturing plant towns and urban areas encouraged new types of local area and character. Laborers frequently lived in closeness to each other and shaped social bonds inside the setting of their common work encounters. The processing plant framework made a feeling of aggregate personality among laborers, laying the preparation for worker's organizations and laborers' developments. These associations looked to advocate for the freedoms of laborers, work on working circumstances, and address issues of pay imbalance.

The development of early production lines additionally had expansive ramifications for society and culture. The large scale manufacturing of merchandise, worked with by motorization and centralization, carried a wide cluster of items to a more extensive crowd. This peculiarity brought about buyer culture, changing ways of life and utilization designs. The accessibility of a rising assortment of merchandise prompted a change in how people apparent their requirements and wants, making way for the cutting edge customer driven economy.

Furthermore, the production line framework fundamentally influenced the regular habitat. The expanded utilization of petroleum derivatives, like coal, to control modern machines added to more significant levels of air contamination. The natural outcomes of industrialization, including air and water contamination, deforestation, and living space annihilation, started to arise as serious worries. Early processing plants were, in numerous ways, at the very front of the ecological difficulties related with industrialization.

The development of early plants was not without its difficulties and debates. Work questions, strikes, and clashes between plant proprietors and laborers were normal as laborers looked for better working circumstances and fair wages. Manufacturing plants were frequently reprimanded for their unfavorable effect on the climate and general wellbeing. Moreover, the centralization of financial power in the possession of manufacturing plant proprietors brought up issues about pay imbalance and laborers' privileges.

Regardless, the production line framework was a main thrust behind the monetary and innovative advancement that portrayed the Modern Upheaval. It established the groundwork for current modern economies and laid out the standards of automation, centralization, and large scale manufacturing that keep on molding this present reality. The early plants addressed a seismic change in the manner merchandise were delivered, affecting the economy as well as the structure holding the system together, culture, and the connection among people and their current circumstance. The development of plants was a basic achievement in the walk of progress and development that characterizes present day modern civilization.

3.2 The Impact of the British Industrial Revolution

The English Modern Unrest, which started in the late eighteenth hundred years and reached out into the nineteenth hundred years, remains as a turning point in mankind's set of experiences. It denoted a significant change in monetary, mechanical, and cultural designs, catapulting England into the cutting edge age and impacting the direction of worldwide turn of events. The extensive effect of the Modern Transformation contacted each aspect of human life, from work and creation to culture, society, and the climate.

One of the main outcomes of the English Modern Upset was the change of work and creation. Automation, the division of work, and the centralization of creation in plants re-imagined the idea of work. Gifted craftsmans and little studios gave way to the plant framework, where apparatus took over many work escalated errands, and laborers were relegated particular jobs on sequential construction systems. This shift denoted the introduction of current industry and expanded the proficiency and size of creation essentially.

While processing plants presented a level of employer stability and standard pay, they likewise achieved new difficulties for the working people. Long working hours, low wages, and now and then unforgiving working circumstances were normal in early plants, prompting work developments and laborers' privileges support. Production line discipline and a more unbending work structure stood out from the general independence of independently employed craftsmans and limited scope makers. As industrialization spread, the idea of work itself went through significant change.

Urbanization was an immediate result of the Modern Unrest. As production lines extended and offered business valuable open doors, rustic populaces rushed to urban communities looking for work. The fast development of metropolitan regions changed the transcendently agrarian scenes of numerous social orders into clamoring modern towns and urban areas. This flood of urbanization prompted the advancement of new types of lodging, transportation organizations, and public administrations to oblige the developing metropolitan populace. The structure holding the system together and the design of networks were always adjusted.

The effect of the English Modern Unrest broadened well past financial and cultural changes. It on a very basic level reshaped culture and values. The accessibility of a rising assortment of efficiently manufactured merchandise led to purchaser culture.

People started to see their requirements and wants in an unexpected way, prompting shifts in utilization examples and ways of life. The Modern Upheaval laid the foundation for the cutting edge customer driven economy, wherein the procurement of products turned into a focal component of day to day existence.

The rise of plants and huge scope industry additionally had international repercussions. The quest for natural substances to take care of the consistently developing hardware and the quest for new business sectors for modern items drove European powers to extend their domains through government. This scramble for assets and markets significantly affected the colonized districts, influencing their societies, economies, and social orders. The period of imperialism and colonialism was firmly connected to the monetary and innovative development of the Modern Upset.

Moreover, the Modern Upset essentially changed the indigenous habitat. The expanded utilization of non-renewable energy sources, like coal, to drive modern machines added to more significant levels of air contamination. Ecological outcomes, including air and water contamination, deforestation, and living space annihilation, started to arise as squeezing concerns. The plants, in numerous ways, were at the very front of the natural difficulties related with industrialization.

One of the sweeping and persevering through outcomes of the English Modern Insurgency was the ascent of present day private enterprise. The Modern Transformation gave the system to private responsibility for method for creation and the quest for benefit. Private enterprise turned into the predominant financial framework, stressing contest, development, and the quest for abundance. The benefit thought process filled in as a strong impetus for speculation and mechanical headway, driving financial development.

The effect of the English Modern Unrest was not restricted to England; it affected the worldwide stage. As different countries saw the financial and innovative advancement accomplished by England, they looked to copy its modern model. The dissemination of industrialization to different pieces of Europe and the US during the nineteenth century denoted a worldwide shift toward modern economies. The Modern Transformation turned into a model for improvement that lengthy its impact to virtually every edge of the world.

3.3 Key Milestones in Early Industrialization

The time of early industrialization, spreading over from the late eighteenth to the mid nineteenth hundreds of years, was set apart by a progression of groundbreaking achievements that reshaped economies, social orders, and mechanical scenes. This period, frequently connected with the Modern Upheaval, set up for the cutting edge modern world and presented an influx of developments and changes that keep on influencing our lives today.

The Innovation of the Steam Motor:

At the core of the Modern Transformation was the steam motor, a mechanical wonder that introduced the period of motorization. James Watt's enhancements to the steam motor during the 1760s and 1770s gave a dependable wellspring of mechanical power that could drive hardware. The steam motor changed many ventures, from material creation to transportation, by giving a predictable and strong wellspring of energy. Steam trains and steamships further changed transportation and exchange, extending markets and empowering the development of individuals and products on an extraordinary scale.

The Automation of Material Creation:

One of the earliest and most groundbreaking utilizations of hardware was in the material business. The automation of turning and winding around processes changed material creation. Machines like the turning jenny, power loom, and water outline fundamentally sped up and proficiency of material assembling. This fulfilled the developing need for materials as well as made way for the motorization of different businesses.

The Manufacturing plant Framework:

The development of the processing plant framework denoted an essential change underway techniques. Processing plants concentrated creation, uniting hardware, natural substances, and a developing workforce under one rooftop. This centralization took into account large scale manufacturing, making economies of scale and essentially expanding the amount of merchandise created. The division of work inside manufacturing plants additionally upgraded productivity, with laborers spend significant time in unambiguous undertakings on sequential construction systems. This model turned into a sign of modern creation and added to the fast monetary development of the time.

The Ascent of Modern Private enterprise:

The Modern Upset remained closely connected with the ascent of modern free enterprise. Free enterprise, as a monetary and social framework, accentuated private responsibility for method for creation and the quest for benefit. This structure gave the impetus to business visionaries and industrialists to put resources into new advancements and creation strategies, driving financial extension. The benefit intention turned into a strong impetus for development and the improvement of present day industry.

Urbanization:

The development of modern focuses and the foundation of manufacturing plants filled urbanization as country populaces rushed to urban communities looking for work. The once prevalently agrarian scenes of numerous social orders changed into clamoring modern towns and urban areas. This influx of urbanization prompted the improvement of new types of lodging, transportation organizations, and public administrations to oblige the expanding metropolitan populace. It significantly affected day to day environments, foundation, and social elements.

Work Developments and Laborers' Freedoms:

The progress from customary high quality work to wage work in production lines achieved new difficulties and differences in working circumstances. Laborers frequently confronted extended periods of time, low wages, and unfortunate working environment conditions. Worker's organizations and laborers' developments arose as a reaction to these issues, pushing for further developed privileges and conditions. This period laid the foundation for the cutting edge work development, which keeps on molding work privileges and guidelines.

The Worldwide Extension of Industrialization:

The outcome of industrialization in England enlivened different countries to embrace comparative modern models. Industrialization spread across Europe and to the US during the nineteenth hundred years. This worldwide dispersion of industrialization generally changed economies and social orders around the world, prompting expanded interconnectedness, exchange, and financial development.

Social and Social Change:

The Modern Upheaval presented massive changes in culture and society. The large scale manufacturing of merchandise, alongside the ascent of shopper culture, changed ways of life and utilization designs. The accessibility of a wide cluster of items molded the manner in which individuals saw their necessities and wants. The rise of industrial facility towns and the arrangement of trade guilds cultivated new types of local area and aggregate personality.

Natural Effect:

The Modern Upheaval additionally had expansive ramifications for the regular habitat. The expanded utilization of petroleum products, like coal, to control modern apparatus prompted more elevated levels of air contamination. Ecological worries, including air and water contamination, deforestation, and territory obliteration, started to arise as major problems. Early processing plants were frequently at the front of ecological difficulties related with industrialization.

The Effect on Government:

The requirement for unrefined substances to fuel modern machines and the quest for new business sectors for modern items drove European powers to grow their domains through government. Colonialism had significant ramifications for the colonized locales, influencing their societies, economies, and social orders. The time of imperialism was firmly connected to the monetary and innovative development of the Modern Transformation.

The introduction of huge scope industry addresses a urgent crossroads in mankind's set of experiences. It denoted a basic change in the manner social orders coordinated their monetary exercises, reshaped the idea of work, and reformed the worldwide economy. This change, frequently alluded to as the Modern Upheaval, had significant and sweeping outcomes that keep on affecting our present reality.

The Modern Upset, which started in the late eighteenth 100 years in England and spread to different regions of the planet, was portrayed by a progression of mechanical developments and changes underway techniques. One of the key factors that powered this modern change was the creation and arrangement of hardware, like the turning jenny and the steam motor. These machines, fueled by steam and later power, could perform undertakings with more prominent speed and proficiency than human work alone. The motorization of enterprises like materials and mining prompted a critical expansion underway limit, bringing about the introduction of huge scope industry.

The material business assumed a focal part in the beginning phases of industrialization. Advancements in material apparatus, similar to the turning jenny and the power loom, reformed the development of fabric. These machines automated the work concentrated cycles of turning and winding around, radically diminishing the time and cost expected to deliver materials. Subsequently, the material business could now create merchandise at a scale previously unheard of, fulfilling the developing need for reasonable dress and textures.

The shift to huge scope industry achieved significant changes in the idea of work. Customary house enterprises, where creation was completed in little, decentralized studios, started to give way to the manufacturing plant framework. Manufacturing plants united huge quantities of laborers under one rooftop, where they worked hardware in a planned and concentrated way. This shift from scattered, frequently family-based creation to incorporated, motorized manufacturing plants had huge social and financial outcomes.

One of the most remarkable impacts of the industrialization of work was the ascent of pay work. As production lines extended and the interest for work expanded, laborers progressively ended up utilized by plant proprietors and paid ordinary wages in return for their work. This shift denoted a huge takeoff from the previous act of craftsmans and craftspeople who worked freely and sold their completed products straightforwardly to shoppers.

The plant framework additionally presented the division of work, where laborers were relegated explicit assignments inside the creation cycle. This specialization further developed productivity and took into consideration more fast and practical creation. Be that as it may, it likewise prompted a downgrading of individual craftsmanship, as laborers became pinions in a bigger modern machine, performing dreary and frequently tedious undertakings. This change in work designs had huge social ramifications, as customary abilities were supplanted by manufacturing plant occupations that necessary less preparation and were frequently less talented.

The change of work and the ascent of huge scope industry made significant social and segment impacts. As individuals moved from provincial regions to metropolitan focuses looking for business, urban areas and towns experienced quick populace development. This urbanization achieved new difficulties, including stuffing, deficient lodging, and general medical problems.

The change to production line work likewise affected relational peculiarities, as it frequently required the work of ladies and youngsters, remembering for dangerous and requesting position, to enhance family earnings.

The approach of enormous scope industry likewise reshaped monetary designs. Private enterprise, as a monetary framework, turned out to be progressively predominant. Processing plant proprietors and entrepreneurs put resources into hardware and the method for creation, looking for benefits through the extension of their organizations. The gathering of capital assumed a focal part in driving further industrialization and monetary development. This shift to an entrepreneur framework, where products were delivered for the market and not exclusively for nearby utilization, sped up monetary turn of events and interconnection on a worldwide scale.

The accessibility of huge scope industry and automated creation likewise prompted expanded worldwide exchange and the globalization of business sectors. Industrialized countries looked to extend their span by delivering merchandise for trade, while recently industrializing nations started to take on comparable methodologies to find their further developed partners. The development of exchange and the development of products across borders turned into a main thrust for monetary development and the making of riches.

One more critical part of the introduction of enormous scope industry was the effect on the climate. The expanded utilization of coal, steam motors, and later, power, for modern cycles prompted the development of the petroleum derivative industry. This, thusly, brought about expanded outflows of ozone harming substances and contamination. The quick industrialization of urban areas had adverse results for air and water quality, frequently prompting general medical conditions.

The Modern Unrest additionally achieved advancements in transportation and correspondence. The improvement of the steam train and the development of rail lines upset the development of individuals and products, making it quicker and more proficient. This extension of transportation networks worked with exchange and considered the circulation of merchandise on a scale beforehand incredible. Moreover, the message and later the phone changed significant distance correspondence, associating individuals and organizations across tremendous distances.

The effect of huge scope industry reached out past monetary and social domains; it had significant political results too. As industrialization advanced, it powered the development of the average workers and the ascent of work developments. Laborers, who were frequently exposed to unfortunate working circumstances and low wages, started to sort out and request better treatment and work freedoms. This prompted the rise of worker's guilds and, in the end, work regulation that planned to safeguard the freedoms of laborers and work on their functioning circumstances.

Notwithstanding work developments, the Modern Insurgency likewise had suggestions for political philosophies. It added to the development of communism and socialism as reactions to the apparent imbalances and shameful acts of entrepreneur modern culture. The works of masterminds like Karl Marx and Friedrich Engels studied the double-dealing of work in the entrepreneur framework and supported for a more impartial circulation of riches and influence.

The introduction of huge scope industry likewise had expansive results on a worldwide scale. Industrialized countries, especially European powers, started to grow their realms, looking to get assets and markets for their modern items. This drive for magnificent extension had significant international ramifications, including the colonization of enormous pieces of Africa and Asia. It likewise set up for international contentions and clashes, which in the end finished in the universal conflicts of the twentieth 100 years.

The Modern Upheaval was not a straight and uniform interaction. Its effect shifted across various nations and districts, contingent upon elements like accessible assets, government approaches, and social circumstances. For instance, while England drove the way in early industrialization, different countries, including the US, Germany, and Japan, in the long run got up to speed and became modern forces to be reckoned with by their own doing.

The introduction of enormous scope industry addresses a critical crossroads in mankind's set of experiences. It denoted a basic change in the manner social orders coordinated their financial exercises, reshaped the idea of work, and upset the worldwide economy. This change, frequently alluded to as the Modern Transformation, had significant and extensive results that keep on affecting our present reality.

The Modern Unrest, which started in the late eighteenth 100 years in England and spread to different regions of the planet, was described by a progression of mechanical developments and changes underway strategies. One of the key factors that filled this modern change was the innovation and arrangement of hardware, like the turning jenny and the steam motor. These machines, fueled by steam and later power, could perform undertakings with more prominent speed and proficiency than human work alone. The motorization of businesses like materials and mining prompted a critical expansion underway limit, bringing about the introduction of enormous scope industry.

The material business assumed a focal part in the beginning phases of industrialization. Developments in material hardware, similar to the turning jenny and the power loom, reformed the creation of fabric. These machines automated the work concentrated cycles of turning and winding around, radically diminishing the time and cost expected to deliver materials. Thus, the material business could now create merchandise at a scale previously unheard of, fulfilling the developing need for reasonable dress and textures.

The shift to enormous scope industry achieved significant changes in the idea of work. Conventional cabin enterprises, where creation was done in little, decentralized studios, started to give way to the processing plant framework. Manufacturing plants united enormous quantities of laborers under one rooftop, where they worked hardware in a planned and concentrated way. This shift from scattered, frequently family-based creation to unified, automated industrial facilities had huge social and monetary results.

One of the most striking impacts of the industrialization of work was the ascent of compensation work. As manufacturing plants extended and the interest for work expanded, laborers progressively ended up utilized by production line proprietors and paid standard wages in return for their work. This shift denoted a critical takeoff from the previous act of craftsmans and craftspeople who worked freely and sold their completed products straightforwardly to buyers.

The industrial facility framework likewise presented the division of work, where laborers were doled out unambiguous undertakings inside the creation cycle. This specialization further developed productivity and took into consideration more quick and savvy creation. Notwithstanding, it likewise prompted a downgrading of individual craftsmanship, as laborers became pinions in a bigger modern machine, performing tedious and frequently dull errands. This change in work designs had huge social ramifications, as customary abilities were supplanted by processing plant occupations that expected less preparation and were frequently less talented.

The change of work and the ascent of huge scope industry made significant social and segment impacts. As individuals moved from provincial regions to metropolitan focuses looking for work, urban areas and towns experienced fast populace development. This urbanization achieved new difficulties, including stuffing, insufficient lodging, and general medical problems. The progress to processing plant work likewise affected relational peculiarities, as it frequently required the work of ladies and kids, remembering for risky and requesting position, to enhance family earnings.

The appearance of huge scope industry additionally reshaped monetary designs. Private enterprise, as a financial framework, turned out to be progressively prevailing. Manufacturing plant proprietors and entrepreneurs put resources into apparatus and the method for creation, looking for benefits through the development of their organizations. The collection of capital assumed a focal part in driving further industrialization and monetary development. This shift to an industrialist framework, where products were created for the market and not exclusively for neighborhood utilization, sped up monetary turn of events and interconnection on a worldwide scale.

The accessibility of enormous scope industry and motorized creation likewise prompted expanded worldwide exchange and the globalization of business sectors.

Industrialized countries looked to extend their range by creating merchandise for send out, while recently industrializing nations started to take on comparative methodologies to find their further developed partners. The extension of exchange and the development of products across borders turned into a main thrust for financial development and the making of riches.

One more critical part of the introduction of huge scope industry was the effect on the climate. The expanded utilization of coal, steam motors, and later, power, for modern cycles prompted the development of the petroleum product industry. This, thus, brought about expanded outflows of ozone depleting substances and contamination. The quick industrialization of urban areas had adverse results for air and water quality, frequently prompting general medical issues.

The Modern Upset additionally achieved developments in transportation and correspondence. The improvement of the steam train and the development of rail lines changed the development of individuals and merchandise, making it quicker and more productive. This extension of transportation networks worked with exchange and considered the circulation of merchandise on a scale beforehand inconceivable. Likewise, the message and later the phone changed significant distance correspondence, interfacing individuals and organizations across immense distances.

The effect of enormous scope industry stretched out past financial and social domains; it had significant political results too. As industrialization advanced, it energized the development of the working people and the ascent of work developments. Laborers, who were frequently exposed to unfortunate working circumstances and low wages, started to arrange and request better treatment and work privileges. This prompted the rise of worker's organizations and, in the long run, work regulation that meant to safeguard the freedoms of laborers and work on their functioning circumstances.

Notwithstanding work developments, the Modern Transformation likewise had suggestions for political philosophies. It added to the development of communism and socialism as reactions to the apparent disparities and treacheries of entrepreneur modern culture. The works of scholars like Karl Marx and Friedrich Engels evaluated the double-dealing of work in the entrepreneur framework and pushed for a more evenhanded circulation of riches and influence.

The introduction of enormous scope industry likewise had extensive results on a worldwide scale. Industrialized countries, especially European powers, started to grow their realms, trying to get assets and markets for their modern items. This drive for majestic extension had significant international ramifications, including the colonization of huge pieces of Africa and Asia. It additionally set up for international competitions and clashes, which at last finished in the universal conflicts of the twentieth hundred years.

The Modern Upset was not a straight and uniform interaction. Its effect fluctuated across various nations and locales, contingent upon elements like accessible assets, government approaches, and social circumstances. For instance, while England drove the way in early industrialization, different countries, including the US, Germany, and Japan, at last got up to speed and became modern forces to be reckoned with by their own doing.

Chapter 4

Pioneering Industrialists

The time of early industrialization, spreading over from the late eighteenth to the mid nineteenth hundreds of years, was set apart by a progression of groundbreaking achievements that reshaped economies, social orders, and innovative scenes. This time, frequently connected with the Modern Upset, set up for the cutting edge modern world and presented a rush of developments and changes that keep on influencing our lives today.

The Creation of the Steam Motor:

At the core of the Modern Upset was the steam motor, a mechanical wonder that introduced the period of motorization. James Watt's upgrades to the steam motor during the 1760s and 1770s gave a dependable wellspring of mechanical power that could drive hardware. The steam motor changed a great many enterprises, from material creation to transportation, by giving a predictable and strong wellspring of energy. Steam trains and steamships further altered transportation and exchange, extending markets and empowering the development of individuals and products on an extraordinary scale.

The Motorization of Material Creation:

One of the earliest and most extraordinary utilizations of hardware was in the material business. The automation of turning and winding around processes altered material creation. Machines like the turning jenny, power loom, and water outline essentially sped up and productivity of material assembling. This satisfied the developing need for materials as well as made way for the automation of different businesses.

The Manufacturing plant Framework:

The development of the plant framework denoted a vital change underway techniques. Plants concentrated creation, uniting hardware, unrefined components, and a developing workforce under one rooftop. This centralization took into account large scale manufacturing, making economies of scale and fundamentally expanding the amount of products created. The division of work inside manufacturing plants additionally upgraded proficiency, with laborers having some expertise in unambiguous undertakings on mechanical production systems. This model turned into a sign of modern creation and added to the fast monetary development of the period.

The Ascent of Modern Private enterprise:

The Modern Upset remained closely connected with the ascent of modern private enterprise. Free enterprise, as a monetary and social framework, accentuated private responsibility for method for creation and the quest for benefit.

This system gave the motivating force to business people and industrialists to put resources into new advances and creation techniques, driving monetary extension. The benefit intention turned into a strong impetus for development and the improvement of present day industry.

Urbanization:

The development of modern focuses and the foundation of manufacturing plants energized urbanization as rustic populaces ran to urban areas looking for business. The once dominatingly agrarian scenes of numerous social orders changed into clamoring modern towns and urban areas. This influx of urbanization prompted the improvement of new types of lodging, transportation organizations, and public administrations to oblige the expanding metropolitan populace. It significantly affected everyday environments, framework, and social elements.

Work Developments and Laborers' Freedoms:

The progress from conventional distinctive work to wage work in plants achieved new difficulties and abberations in working circumstances. Laborers frequently confronted extended periods, low wages, and unfortunate working environment conditions. Worker's organizations and laborers' developments arose as a reaction to these issues, supporting for further developed privileges and conditions. This period laid the preparation for the cutting edge work development, which keeps on molding work privileges and guidelines.

The Worldwide Development of Industrialization:

The outcome of industrialization in England motivated different countries to embrace comparable modern models. Industrialization spread across Europe and to the US during the nineteenth 100 years. This worldwide dispersion of industrialization generally changed economies and social orders around the world, prompting expanded interconnectedness, exchange, and monetary development.

Social and Social Change:

The Modern Unrest presented huge changes in culture and society. The large scale manufacturing of products, alongside the ascent of purchaser culture, changed ways of life and utilization designs. The accessibility of a wide cluster of items formed the manner in which individuals saw their requirements and wants. The rise of processing plant towns and the development of worker's guilds encouraged new types of local area and aggregate character.

Natural Effect:

The Modern Transformation likewise had broad ramifications for the common habitat. The expanded utilization of non-renewable energy sources, like coal, to drive modern apparatus prompted more significant levels of air contamination. Natural worries, including air and water contamination, deforestation, and living space annihilation, started to arise as major problems. Early plants were frequently at the front of natural difficulties related with industrialization.

The Effect on Government:

The requirement for natural substances to fuel modern machines and the quest for new business sectors for modern items drove European powers to extend their domains through colonialism. Government had significant ramifications for the colonized districts, influencing their societies, economies, and social orders. The period of imperialism was firmly connected to the financial and innovative extension of the Modern Upheaval.

4.1 Profiles of Visionaries and Entrepreneurs

The Modern Upheaval, an extraordinary period that reshaped economies and social orders, owed quite a bit of progress to spearheading industrialists drove development, put resources into innovation, and fabricated domains of industry. These visionary business people assumed a critical part in propelling industrialization and molding the cutting edge world. Here, we investigate the commitments and traditions of probably the most persuasive spearheading industrialists of the time.

James Watt (1736-1819):

James Watt, a Scottish specialist and innovator, is famous for his upgrades to the steam motor. His advancements, which incorporated the different condenser and the sun-and-planet gear, fundamentally expanded the motor's productivity and dependability. Watt's steam motor turned into a basic part of early manufacturing plants and transportation frameworks, controlling hardware and trains. His commitments changed modern creation and laid out the steam motor as a symbol of the Modern Upset.

Richard Arkwright (1732-1792):

Richard Arkwright, frequently alluded to as the "Father of the Modern Upset," was a critical figure in the motorization of material creation. He designed the water outline, a turning machine that created cotton string at a lot higher rate than physical work. Arkwright's water-fueled manufacturing plants, outfitted with his licensed machines, denoted a defining moment in the material business. His developments expanded the proficiency of material creation as well as established the groundwork for the manufacturing plant framework and large scale manufacturing.

Samuel Slater (1768-1835):

Samuel Slater, an English settler to the US, assumed an essential part in carrying industrialization to America. He was instrumental in laying out the primary material plant in the US, using the information he had obtained working in the material business in Britain. Slater's factory in Pawtucket, Rhode Island, denoted the start of the American modern upheaval and set up for the development of assembling in the US.

Robert Owen (1771-1858):

Robert Owen was a Welsh industrialist and social reformer known for his dynamic thoughts on specialists' government assistance and social obligation. He dealt with the New Lanark cotton plants in Scotland, where he executed a progression of work and social changes, including worked on working circumstances, schooling for kids, and lodging for laborers.

Owen's endeavors at New Lanark filled in as a model for early friendly tests in modern networks and laid the basis for later work changes.

George Stephenson (1781-1848):

George Stephenson, frequently viewed as the "Father of the Rail routes," made huge commitments to the advancement of steam trains and rail lines. His designing developments, including the plan of the train motor "Rocket," changed transportation and assumed a critical part in the extension of railroads. Stephenson's trains gave a quicker and more productive method for moving merchandise and individuals, interfacing urban communities and districts and working with financial development.

Eli Whitney (1765-1825):

Eli Whitney, an American innovator and maker, is most popular for his creation of the cotton gin. The cotton gin automated the most common way of isolating cotton filaments from seeds, making cotton creation more proficient and beneficial. Whitney's creation significantly affected the cotton business in the southern US and prompted the development of cotton development, which, thus, filled the development of bondage and the cotton economy.

Isambard Realm Brunel (1806-1859):

Isambard Realm Brunel was an English designer known for his creative work in different fields, including common and mechanical designing. His commitments to the development of the Incomparable Western Rail line, the Incomparable Western Dockyard, and the Incomparable Western Steamship Organization, among others, assumed a vital part in propelling transportation and designing during the Modern Upheaval. Brunel's plans and undertakings made a permanent imprint on the English foundation.

Andrew Carnegie (1835-1919):

Andrew Carnegie was a Scottish-American industrialist and humanitarian who assumed a focal part in the development of the American steel industry. He was a trailblazer in vertical joining, claiming and controlling each part of the steel creation process, from unrefined components to transportation. Carnegie's imaginative way to deal with steel creation, combined with his magnanimous endeavors in regions like training and libraries, left an enduring heritage in both industry and society.

John D. Rockefeller (1839-1937):

John D. Rockefeller, an American industry mogul and donor, is most popular for his part in the improvement of the petrol business. Through his organization, Standard Oil, Rockefeller accomplished a close syndication on the oil business in the US. His forceful business strategies and methodologies, including vertical joining and trust arrangement, changed the oil business and set up for antitrust regulation in the US.

Thomas Edison (1847-1931):

Thomas Edison, an American designer and money manager, was a trailblazer in the improvement of power and the light. He held more than 1,000 licenses, covering many innovations, from the phonograph to the movie camera. Edison's work in electrical designing and his foundation of the Overall Electric Organization added to the far and wide reception of power and the development of the electrical business.

These spearheading industrialists, each in their one of a kind way, assumed a huge part in molding the Modern Unrest and the ensuing improvements that changed the world. Their developments and business discernment drove progress and set up for the cutting edge modern age, leaving an enduring heritage in the domains of innovation, industry, and society.

4.2 Their Contributions to India's Industrial Growth

India's excursion toward industrialization has been molded by the commitments of various visionaries, business people, and industrialists who assumed essential parts in driving the country's monetary development and advancement. These people reformed different businesses as well as left an enduring effect on the direction of India's modern scene. Here, we investigate the commitments of a portion of the vital figures in India's modern history.

Jamsetji Goodbye (1839-1904):

Jamsetji Goodbye, frequently alluded to as the "Father of Indian Industry," was a visionary industrialist who established the groundwork for India's modern turn of events. He laid out the Goodbye Gathering, which would develop to become one of India's biggest and most enhanced combinations. Goodbye's spearheading endeavors incorporated the foundation of the Goodbye Iron and Steel Organization (presently Goodbye Steel) in 1907, India's originally coordinated steel plant. This undeniable a critical jump in India's modern capacity and laid the preparation for future modern development. Goodbye's accentuation on training and social government assistance likewise left an enduring heritage, including the establishing of the Indian Organization of Science in Bangalore.

Ardeshir Godrej (1868-1936) and Pirojsha Godrej (1882-1972):

Ardeshir and Pirojsha Godrej, pioneers behind the Godrej Gathering, were instrumental in driving modern development in India. They spearheaded the improvement of locks and safes, denoting the start of Godrej's excursion into assembling. Over the long run, the organization expanded into a large number of enterprises, including shopper merchandise, land, and synthetics. The Godrej Gathering's obligation to quality and development has made it a commonly recognized name in India, and its commitments to India's modern scene keep on being critical.

J.R.D. Goodbye (1904-1993):

J.R.D. Goodbye, the child of Ratanji Dadabhoy Goodbye, assumed a critical part in growing the Goodbye Gathering's modern impression.

He was a visionary chief who managed the broadening of the Goodbye combination into different areas, including flight, steel, and cars. Goodbye Engines, under his administration, presented the famous Goodbye Indica, India's most memorable natively created traveler vehicle. His emphasis on advancement and obligation to social government assistance prompted the foundation of establishments like Goodbye Organization of Sociologies and the Goodbye Dedication Center.

Dhirubhai Ambani (1932-2002):

Dhirubhai Ambani, the pioneer behind Dependence Enterprises, is generally perceived for changing India's material industry and laying out one of the biggest and most persuasive business aggregates in the country. Under his initiative, Dependence ventured into assorted areas, including petrochemicals, refining, media communications, and retail. Ambani's business sharpness, accentuation on mass customer claim, and steady quest for development made Dependence a critical player in India's modern scene.

Ratan Goodbye:

Ratan Goodbye, the previous director of the Goodbye Gathering, proceeded with the tradition of his ancestors and assumed a significant part in the gathering's extension and expansion. Under his authority, the Goodbye Gathering extended its worldwide presence, with acquisitions in areas like steel, auto, and data innovation. The acquisition of Puma Land Meanderer in 2008 denoted a critical achievement in Goodbye's worldwide development. Ratan Goodbye's obligation to development, corporate social obligation, and moral strategic policies has made the Goodbye Gathering an image of greatness in Indian industry.

Anand Mahindra:

Anand Mahindra, the director of the Mahindra Gathering, is perceived for his endeavors in growing the gathering's worldwide impression and broadening its financial matters. The Mahindra Gathering, at first known for its farm vehicles and car business, has stretched out its presence to different areas, including aviation, data innovation, and monetary administrations. Mahindra's attention on maintainability and development lines up with India's cutting edge modern necessities.

Narayana Murthy:

N.R. Narayana Murthy, the prime supporter of Infosys, is a conspicuous figure in India's data innovation (IT) industry. His initiative at Infosys, a worldwide IT benefits and counseling organization, added to India's development as a worldwide IT center point. Infosys assumed a urgent part in India's product administrations send out industry and assisted shape the nation's situation in the worldwide innovation with finishing.

Azim Premji:

Azim Premji, the director of Wipro, is one more outstanding figure in India's IT area. Under his administration, Wipro extended its IT administrations and programming arrangements universally. His obligation to altruism, exemplified by the Azim Premji Establishment, shows the double spotlight on business development and social obligation.

Kiran Mazumdar-Shaw:

Kiran Mazumdar-Shaw, the pioneer behind Biocon, made critical commitments to the biotechnology and drug businesses in India. Biocon, one of India's biggest biopharmaceutical organizations, is known for its work in creating reasonable and imaginative medical services arrangements. Mazumdar-Shaw's spearheading endeavors have situated Biocon as a worldwide forerunner in biotechnology and biosimilars.

Mukesh Ambani:

Mukesh Ambani, the executive and overseeing head of Dependence Enterprises, has proceeded with the tradition of his dad, Dhirubhai Ambani, by growing the organization's presence in the petrochemicals, refining, media communications, and retail areas. Dependence Jio's problematic section into the Indian broadcast communications market denoted a huge achievement, changing the computerized scene in the country.

These spearheading industrialists, alongside numerous others, play played instrumental parts in forming India's modern development and adding to the country's financial turn of events. Their pioneering soul, obligation to development, and vision for modern extension have changed different areas as well as made India a critical player in the worldwide modern scene. Their heritages keep on affecting the eventual fate of India's industrialization and development.

4.3 Challenges and Triumphs of Early Industrialists

The early industrialists of the eighteenth and nineteenth hundreds of years confronted a novel arrangement of difficulties and wins as they explored the unfamiliar waters of industrialization. These spearheading business people assumed a crucial part in molding the Modern Transformation and, in doing as such, changed economies, social orders, and the actual idea of work. While they accomplished exceptional victories, they likewise experienced various snags and issues in their quest for development and riches.

Wins:

Mechanical Development:

One of the main victories of early industrialists was their ability to drive mechanical development. They saddled the capability of developments like the steam motor, automated weavers, power-driven hardware to change different businesses. These developments worked on the effectiveness of creation as well as established the groundwork for present day assembling and transportation frameworks.

Pioneering Vision:

Early industrialists had striking pioneering vision. They been able to distinguish open doors and change them into flourishing undertakings. Trailblazers like Richard Arkwright and James Watt perceived the capability of motorized material creation and the steam motor, separately. Their visionary reasoning and eagerness to put resources into these innovations were key drivers of industrialization.

Monetary Development and Occupation Creation:

The industrialists of the period contributed essentially to financial development and occupation creation. The extension of manufacturing plants and automated creation processes prompted expanded yield, which, thusly, drove monetary turn of events. These improvements gave business potential open doors to a developing labor force, particularly in metropolitan regions, where industrialization was concentrated.

Abundance Aggregation:

Numerous early industrialists made critical abundance and progress. Business people like Andrew Carnegie and John D. Rockefeller amassed fortunes through their endeavors in steel and oil, separately. Their abundance assumed a vital part in forming generosity, as they became noticeable promoters of training, medical care, and other social causes.

Worldwide Development:

A few early industrialists extended their tasks worldwide, adding to the improvement of global business sectors and exchange. The foundation of organizations in states and far off locales worked with the trading of merchandise and assets, further energizing monetary development. This worldwide development set out open doors for advancement and coordinated effort on an overall scale.

Challenges:

Work Conditions:

Early manufacturing plants were frequently scrutinized for their unfortunate work conditions. Laborers confronted long working hours, low wages, and hazardous working environments. The processing plant framework presented another division of work, which prompted dreary and redundant assignments on mechanical production systems. Worker's organizations and laborers' developments arose because of these difficulties, upholding for worked on working circumstances and laborers' freedoms.

Ecological Effect:

The fast industrialization of the period had antagonistic ramifications for the climate. The expanded utilization of petroleum products to control modern hardware added to air contamination, deforestation, and territory annihilation. Early processing plants were related with natural difficulties, and the drawn out environmental effect turned into a critical concern.

Social Incongruities:

The industrialization cycle made huge abberations in the public eye. While certain industrialists amassed massive riches, numerous laborers battled to earn a living wage. Pay imbalance extended, prompting social pressures and monetary differences that endure right up to the present day.

Kid Work:

Kid work was a far and wide issue during the beginning phases of industrialization. Numerous kids were utilized in manufacturing plants, frequently exposed to cruel circumstances and long working hours. The double-dealing of kid work was a profoundly upsetting part of industrialization and turned into a focal point of change endeavors.

Urbanization:

The fast urbanization coming about because of industrialization achieved huge difficulties with regards to lodging, disinfection, and foundation. Urban communities and towns, caught off guard for the convergence of country transients, attempted to give sufficient day to day environments and public administrations.

Government and Expansionism:

The quest for unrefined components and new business sectors to fuel modern hardware and development prompted the colonization of unfamiliar grounds by European powers. Government had broad results on the way of life, economies, and social orders of colonized locales, raising moral and international issues.

Innovative Disturbance:

While mechanical development was a victory, it likewise presented difficulties. Customary craftsmans and specialists found their abilities and occupations compromised by automated creation. The progress to motorization frequently prompted work uprooting and social disturbance in networks dependent on customary craftsmanship.

Moral Situations:

The quest for benefit frequently prompted moral situations for early industrialists. Strategic approaches like trusts and restraining infrastructures, utilized by figures like John D. Rockefeller, raised worries about market contest and reasonableness. Moral contemplations in business and industry were subjects of progressing discussion and change.

The historical backdrop of present day industrialization is a story of development, desire, and creativity, with spearheading industrialists at its center. These visionaries assumed a urgent part in reshaping the world's monetary and social scene during the eighteenth and nineteenth hundreds of years. Their groundbreaking endeavors altered businesses as well as established the groundwork for the cutting edge worldwide economy. In this account, we will investigate the lives and commitments of a few key industrialists, looking at the effect of their developments, their ways to deal with business, and the enduring heritage they left on society.

Quite possibly of the most noticeable figure in the beginning phases of the Modern Transformation was Sir Richard Arkwright. His creation of the water outline in the late eighteenth century denoted a defining moment in material assembling. This progressive gadget saddled water ability to motorize the turning of cotton, empowering a huge expansion underway effectiveness.

Arkwright's industrial facility framework, with its incorporated and motorized approach, set a trend for present day fabricating. His developments not just expanded the efficiency of the material business yet in addition had significant cultural ramifications, including the development of metropolitan focuses and the change of the labor force.

Arkwright's contemporary and individual material head honcho, Samuel Slater, had a huge effect on industrialization in the US. Frequently alluded to as the "Father of the American Modern Transformation," Slater retained the subtleties of Arkwright's water outline innovation and, with the assistance of his colleague Moses Brown, effectively duplicated it in Pawtucket, Rhode Island. Slater's variation of English modern strategies to the American setting prompted the quick development of material factories and the introduction of the American modern framework. His commitment was instrumental in laying the foundation for the US's development as a worldwide monetary force to be reckoned with.

One more spearheading industrialist of the period was James Watt, whose upgrades to the steam motor extraordinarily affected different businesses. His development of the consolidating steam motor, which successfully outfit the force of steam to perform mechanical work, assumed a significant part in driving processing plants, trains, and ships. Watt's motor supplanted conventional wellsprings of force as well as prompted expanded proficiency and efficiency in different applications. His developments lastingly affected transportation, fabricating, and the general development of modern economies.

As industrialization progressed, the development of railways arose as a vital driver of financial turn of events. George Stephenson, known as the "Father of Rail lines," altered transportation with his plan and execution of the steam train.

Stephenson's "Rocket," worked in 1829, was the world's most memorable effective steam-controlled train and denoted a critical headway in rail line innovation. The improvement of railroads not just worked with the development of merchandise and individuals yet in addition associated districts and cultivated monetary development for a gigantic scope.

The Modern Upset was not exclusively determined by the material and transportation businesses. Iron and steel creation assumed a crucial part in the improvement of framework and hardware. One of the vital figures in this area was Andrew Carnegie. Naturally introduced to an unfortunate family in Scotland, Carnegie emigrated to the US and fabricated an immense domain in the steel business. His business insight and vertical mix technique permitted him to control all parts of steel creation, from mining to assembling to transportation. Carnegie's developments in the steel business helped lay the basis for the development of scaffolds, structures, and rail lines, molding the actual scene of the advanced world.

The oil business additionally experienced critical change during the Modern Upset, on account of people like John D. Rockefeller. Rockefeller, the pioneer behind Standard Oil, was an expert of corporate union and even reconciliation. His organization turned into a behemoth in the oil business, controlling a significant part of the worldwide oil market.

Through forceful strategic policies and inventive planned operations, Standard Oil accomplished unmatched economies of scale, radically lessening the expense of oil creation and dispersion. Rockefeller's impact reached out past business, as he assumed a focal part in molding the early oil industry and its guideline, eventually adding to the development of antitrust regulations.

The late nineteenth century saw the ascent of another modern monster, Thomas Edison. Known as the "Wizard of Menlo Park," Edison held more than 1,000 licenses and was a trailblazer in the fields of power and broadcast communications. He is generally prestigious for imagining the reasonable brilliant light, which altered indoor lighting and established the groundwork for current electrical frameworks. Edison's work on the phonograph and movies likewise significantly affected diversion and correspondence, molding the manner in which individuals cooperated with innovation and media.

While these industrialists made striking progress, their accounts were not without discussion. The fast development of businesses frequently came to the detriment of workers. Working circumstances in processing plants and mines were frequently unforgiving, and kid work was pervasive. Work developments and associations emerged because of these difficulties, trying to work on the circumstances and freedoms of laborers. Industrialists like Henry Passage, who spearheaded the mechanical production system and made vehicles reasonable for the general population, confronted analysis for his position on worker's guilds and work rehearses.

India's Industrial Rise

Passage's advancements in assembling and large scale manufacturing upset the auto business. His presentation of the sequential construction system definitely diminished creation times and expenses, making vehicles more reasonable to the overall population. The Model T, Portage's most renowned creation, turned into a symbol of the American car industry and aided shape present day transportation and versatility.

The effect of industrialists reached out past their particular enterprises. Magnanimity and rewarding society turned into a necessary piece of the tradition of numerous industrialists. Andrew Carnegie, for example, was areas of strength for an of "the Good news of Riches," the conviction that the well off had an ethical constraint to involve their fortunes for everyone's benefit. Carnegie financed libraries, instructive foundations, and social focuses, leaving an enduring heritage in the fields of schooling and culture. Moreover, John D. Rockefeller laid out the Rockefeller Establishment, which zeroed in on working on general wellbeing, schooling, and logical examination.

The spearheading industrialists likewise transformed metropolitan turn of events. As businesses developed, so did the requirement for a labor force. Manufacturing plants and factories pulled in individuals from country regions to metropolitan focuses looking for work. This gigantic country to-metropolitan movement prompted the fast extension of urban communities and the improvement of metropolitan foundation.

Industrialists like George Pullman, who planned and assembled the main broadly involved resting vehicle for rail travel, added to the development of transportation and urbanization.

The tradition of spearheading industrialists reaches out to the current day, impacting present day strategic approaches and innovation. The standards of large scale manufacturing and productivity created by figures like Henry Passage keep on forming fabricating processes. Developments in transportation, like the electric vehicle, owe a lot to crafted by early industrialists like Thomas Edison and his peers. Indeed, even the altruistic undertakings started by industrialists like Andrew Carnegie and John D. Rockefeller set up for present day altruism and corporate social obligation.

Chapter 5

India's Industrial Policies

India's modern strategies play had a critical impact in forming the country's modern scene and monetary turn of events. Throughout the long term, these approaches have advanced to adjust to changing worldwide elements, homegrown necessities, and monetary objectives. From the early long stretches of arranged advancement to the later spotlight on progression and globalization, India's modern approaches have tried to adjust different goals, including financial development, confidence, and worldwide intensity.

The Early Long stretches of Modern Preparation:

India's post-freedom modern strategies were at first portrayed by an emphasis on independence and state-drove improvement. The nation took on an arranged economy model, underlining focal preparation, public possession, and import replacement industrialization (ISI). Import replacement was viewed as a way to lessen reliance on unfamiliar products and to support homegrown enterprises.

Key Highlights:

Modern Authorizing: During this period, modern permitting was acquainted with manage the foundation, area, and extension of enterprises. The public authority controlled admittance to assets, innovation, and markets to advance adjusted modern turn of events.

Public Area Predominance: The state assumed a huge part in modern turn of events, with an emphasis on laying out and working enterprises in essential areas, including weighty businesses, framework, and protection. This prompted the production of public area endeavors (PSUs).

Protectionist Exchange Strategies: Import levies and non-duty obstructions were utilized to safeguard homegrown ventures from unfamiliar rivalry. The accentuation was on independence and diminishing the import/export imbalance.

Monopolistic and Prohibitive Guidelines: The administrative climate frequently preferred monopolistic works on, prompting restricted contest and failures in the modern area.

Progression and Monetary Changes:

In the mid 1990s, India went through a change in perspective in its monetary strategies. The public authority sent off a progression of financial changes that expected to change the economy, advance confidential area cooperation, and incorporate India into the worldwide economy. This noticeable the start of a takeoff from the vigorously directed, protectionist modern strategies of the past.

Key Highlights:

Destroying of Modern Authorizing: The course of advancement started with the annulment of the modern permitting system. Businesses were classified into three gatherings: those requiring mandatory permitting, those subject to programmed endorsement, and those held for the public area. Most ventures were moved to the programmed endorsement list, fundamentally diminishing regulatory obstacles for new speculations.

Privatization: The public authority started the privatization of many state-claimed ventures. This cycle planned to further develop proficiency, seriousness, and the nature of administrations in ventures recently overwhelmed by the public area.

Exchange Progression: India diminished import taxes and destroyed non-duty hindrances, making it simpler for unfamiliar products and speculations to enter the Indian market. The nation additionally went into economic deals, prompting more noteworthy financial combination with the worldwide economy.

Unfamiliar Direct Venture (FDI): India opened up different areas to FDI, permitting unfamiliar organizations to put resources into businesses like broadcast communications, retail, and monetary administrations.

Innovation and Advancement: The public authority effectively energized the development of the data innovation and programming administrations industry, which ultimately prompted India turning into a worldwide center for Itself and programming improvement.

Late Modern Approach Structures:

As of late, India has kept on refining its modern approaches, zeroing in on regions, for example, simplicity of carrying on with work, advancement, and economical turn of events. The "Make in India" crusade, sent off in 2014, expected to advance assembling and change India into a worldwide assembling center point.

Key Elements:

Simplicity of Carrying on with Work: The Indian government has done whatever it may take to improve on guidelines, decrease regulatory formality, and establish a more business-accommodating climate to draw in both homegrown and unfamiliar ventures.

Fire up Environment: India has cultivated a flourishing beginning up biological system, with strategies that advance business venture, development, and innovation improvement. Drives like "Startup India" offer help and motivating forces to new organizations.

Manageability and Environmentally friendly power: India is focused on reasonable turn of events and has set aggressive focuses for environmentally friendly power reception. Arrangements empower interest in clean energy, energy productivity, and maintainable assembling rehearses.

Atmanirbhar Bharat (Confident India): Presented in 2020, this arrangement structure looks to make India more independent in basic areas while advancing homegrown assembling and diminishing reliance on imports.

Difficulties and Concerns:

While India's modern arrangements have developed in light of changing financial real factors, there are difficulties and worries that continue:

Foundation Deficiencies: Regardless of endeavors to further develop framework, India actually faces difficulties in regions like transportation, energy, and operations. Insufficient framework can prevent modern development and intensity.

Administrative Intricacy: The administrative climate in India can in any case be complicated and regulatory, prompting postponements and vulnerability for financial backers.

Expertise Improvement: A gifted labor force is fundamental for modern development, yet there is a requirement for greater expertise advancement drives to satisfy the needs of a quickly changing modern scene.

Adjusting Development and Manageability: As India looks to industrialize and develop its economy, it should likewise address natural worries and guarantee that modern improvement is supportable.

Imbalance and Inclusivity: Financial development should be comprehensive and address pay disparity. India's modern arrangements ought to intend to set out open doors and advantages for all portions of society.

Worldwide Rivalry: As India opens up to the worldwide economy, it faces rivalry from different nations, which requires proceeded with endeavors to improve seriousness and development.

5.1 Overview of Government Policies and Reforms

Government strategies and changes assume a basic part in forming the monetary, social, and political scene of a country. These strategies are instrumental in accomplishing various targets, including financial development, social value, ecological maintainability, and worldwide seriousness. The course and viability of government strategies have sweeping results, affecting enterprises, organizations, and the existences of residents. This outline investigates the meaning of government strategies and changes in various parts of a nation's turn of events.

Monetary Arrangements and Changes:

Monetary strategies are a center part of any administration's plan. They intend to deal with the country's financial assets and exercises, drive monetary development, and guarantee monetary soundness. Financial strategies can cover a great many regions, including financial strategy, money related approach, exchange strategy, and modern strategy.

Monetary Approach: Financial arrangements include government choices with respect to tax collection and public spending. State run administrations can utilize monetary approach to impact total interest, control expansion, and asset fundamental administrations like medical care, schooling, and framework. Monetary changes could zero in on charge code improvement, moderate tax collection, or further developing public consumption the executives.

Financial Strategy: Money related approach includes the administration of the cash supply and loan costs to impact expansion, work, and monetary development. National banks assume a key part in carrying out financial strategy. Changes in this space might target national bank autonomy, expansion focusing on, or the utilization of unusual financial devices.

Exchange Strategy: Exchange approaches are fundamental for a country's commitment with the worldwide economy. State run administrations can utilize exchange approaches to safeguard homegrown ventures, advance products, and arrange economic accords. Changes could include exchange progression, lessening taxes, and tending to exchange irregular characteristics.

Modern Approach: Modern strategies expect to encourage the development and advancement of explicit businesses. These arrangements can incorporate appropriations, motivators, and guidelines that target key areas like assembling, innovation, and sustainable power. Modern arrangement changes can include further developing the business climate, smoothing out guidelines, and advancing advancement.

Social Strategies and Changes:

Social strategies address different parts of a country's social prosperity, including schooling, medical services, social wellbeing nets, and destitution decrease. These approaches are fundamental for diminishing imbalance and improving the personal satisfaction for residents.

Instruction Strategy: Schooling approaches oversee the design and financing of schooling systems. Changes in training could include further developing admittance to quality schooling, refreshing educational plans to reflect changing abilities necessities, and growing advanced and remote learning valuable open doors.

Medical care Strategy: Medical care arrangements cover the arrangement of clinical benefits, general wellbeing, and health care coverage. Changes in medical services can plan to grow admittance to mind, further develop medical care foundation, and address general wellbeing challenges.

Social Wellbeing Nets: Social security nets are strategies that offer monetary and social help to weak populaces. Changes in this space could include growing federal retirement aide programs, further developing joblessness benefits, and upgrading help for low-pay families.

Destitution Decrease: Neediness decrease strategies focus on the underlying drivers of destitution, like joblessness, absence of admittance to schooling, and lacking medical services. Changes might zero in on setting out work open doors, supporting private companies, and executing neediness lightening programs.

Ecological Strategies and Changes:

Ecological strategies and changes are fundamental for tending to environmental change, safeguarding biological systems, and advancing economical asset the board. These strategies are vital for relieving the ecological effect of industrialization and monetary development.

Environmental Change Strategy: Environmental change arrangements intend to lessen ozone harming substance outflows and cutoff an Earth-wide temperature boost. Changes in this space could include progressing to clean energy sources, executing carbon valuing systems, and upgrading energy productivity.

Normal Asset The board: Arrangements connected with regular asset the executives center around safeguarding environments, woodlands, water assets, and biodiversity. Changes might include preservation endeavors, feasible woods the executives, and watershed insurance drives.

Squander The executives: Squander the board arrangements address the appropriate removal and reusing of waste materials. Changes can target squander decrease, reusing programs, and naturally mindful garbage removal rehearses.

Worldwide Intensity and Exchange Approaches:

Worldwide seriousness and exchange strategies are basic for a country's investment the worldwide economy. These arrangements influence economic deals, unfamiliar speculation, and the simplicity of carrying on with work.

Economic deals: Economic alliance, like international alliances and territorial exchange settlements, impact a country's exchange relations and admittance to worldwide business sectors. Changes could include haggling new economic deals, reexamining existing ones, or investigating new exchange associations.

Unfamiliar Speculation: Approaches connected with unfamiliar venture mean to draw in unfamiliar capital and innovation. Changes in this space could include changing unfamiliar venture rules, smoothing out endorsement processes, and giving speculation motivations.

Simplicity of Carrying on with Work: Arrangements that work with the simplicity of carrying on with work are fundamental for empowering business and venture. Changes might include diminishing administrative obstacles, working on guidelines, and improving the business climate.

Political and Administration Changes:

Political and administration changes center around improving the working of political foundations, advancing straightforwardness, and fortifying law and order.

A majority rule government and Political Framework: Political changes can envelop changes in discretionary frameworks, party supporting, and political portrayal. Endeavors to upgrade vote based administration might include sacred corrections, appointive changes, and fortifying the legal executive.

Defilement and Straightforwardness: Approaches and changes focusing on debasement and further developing straightforwardness are fundamental for good administration. Changes can incorporate enemy of debasement measures, informant security, and open government drives.

Legal Changes: Legal changes intend to fortify law and order and further develop admittance to equity. Changes could include modernizing the legal framework, lessening case excess, and upgrading legitimate guide administrations.

5.2 The Role of Regulation and Deregulation

Guideline and liberation are fundamental apparatuses in the domain of public strategy and financial aspects, forming the working of businesses, markets, and the more extensive economy. These strategies are much of the time used to find some kind of harmony between guaranteeing fair contest, safeguarding shoppers, and cultivating monetary development. Guideline, which includes government intercession and oversight, is expected to address market disappointments and shield public government assistance, while liberation means to decrease government mediation to support market-driven efficiencies. In this investigation, we dive into the job of guideline and liberation in different areas and their effect on monetary elements.

Guideline:

Guideline alludes to government-forced rules, principles, and oversight intended to oversee and direct financial exercises, enterprises, and markets. The essential goals of guideline are as per the following:

Purchaser Insurance: Guidelines intend to safeguard buyers from risky items, extortion, tricky practices, and monopolistic way of behaving. Customer assurance measures incorporate naming prerequisites, item security norms, and fair rivalry regulations.

Market Rivalry: Guideline is frequently used to advance and save contest inside businesses. Against trust regulations and contest strategies assist with forestalling syndications and anticompetitive works on, guaranteeing that markets stay open and available to different members.

Wellbeing and Security: Administrative bodies set guidelines and lead investigations to guarantee that items and administrations meet wellbeing and wellbeing necessities. Models incorporate sanitation guidelines, work environment wellbeing rules, and drug quality principles.

Ecological Preservation: Natural guidelines are pointed toward safeguarding normal assets, decreasing contamination, and advancing manageability. These guidelines set emanation limits, lay out untamed life insurance measures, and order garbage removal rules.

Monetary Strength: Administrative bodies supervise monetary foundations and markets to keep up with monetary dependability and safeguard purchasers. Banking guidelines, protections regulations, and money related strategies are a portion of the devices utilized for monetary area oversight.

Public Utilities: Guideline is regularly utilized in open utility areas, like power, water, and broadcast communications, to guarantee general access, fair evaluating, and quality assistance arrangement. Controllers set duties, screen administration quality, and direct framework speculations.

Financial Arrangement: National banks carry out financial approaches to direct the cash supply, control expansion, and balance out the economy. These approaches impact loan costs, credit accessibility, and the by and large monetary climate.

Liberation:

Liberation includes the decrease or evacuation of unofficial laws and limitations in different ventures, determined to advance contest, development, and market-driven efficiencies. The critical goals of liberation are as per the following:

Market Proficiency: Liberation looks to take out hindrances to advertise section and diminish government intercession, permitting markets to work all the more productively. Contest between organizations is empowered, prompting further developed items, administrations, and valuing.

Development: Liberation frequently cultivates a climate that empowers advancement and business. Decreased administrative requirements can prompt new market contestants and creative plans of action.

Purchaser Decision: Liberation can improve buyer decision by opening up business sectors to a more extensive cluster of suppliers. Buyers might profit from additional choices, serious estimating, and further developed help quality.

Cost Decrease: Liberation can prompt expense decreases for organizations by disposing of consistence troubles and advancing productive asset distribution. This, thusly, can bring down costs for customers.

Financial Development: Liberation can animate monetary development by liberating organizations from unnecessary administrative noise and permitting them to put resources into extension and advancement.

Influence on Various Areas:

The effect of guideline and liberation fluctuates across various areas of the economy.

Broadcast communications: Liberation in the media communications industry has prompted expanded contest, extended admittance, and mechanical headways.

The separation of monopolistic media communications organizations and the presentation of remote advancements are eminent results of liberation.

Energy: Liberation in the energy area has advanced rivalry in power and flammable gas markets, bringing about cost reserve funds for customers and more noteworthy decision in specialist co-ops.

Transportation: Liberation of the carrier business, with the Carrier Liberation Demonstration of 1978 in the US, prompted lower airfares, more flight choices, and a more cutthroat market. Conversely, some contend that liberation in the shipping business has brought about wellbeing concerns.

Monetary Administrations: The monetary area has seen both guideline and liberation. Guidelines, for example, the Dodd-Honest Money Road Change and Customer Assurance Act, were acquainted with forestall monetary emergencies, while liberation endeavors meant to diminish consistence costs and animate loaning.

Medical care: The medical services area has seen banters over unofficial law. Guidelines in medical services mean to safeguard patient security and guarantee quality consideration, yet they can likewise prompt managerial failures and cost concerns.

Drugs: Administrative oversight in the drug business is fundamental for patient wellbeing and viability. Nonetheless, some contend that unnecessary guidelines might frustrate drug advancement and increment medical care costs.

Difficulties and Contemplations:

Adjusting the jobs of guideline and liberation is an intricate and testing try. Policymakers should think about a few key variables:

Market Disappointment: Guideline is many times vital in instances of market disappointment, like normal imposing business models, externalities, and data deviation, where the market alone can't guarantee ideal results.

Purchaser Insurance: Guaranteeing the security and government assistance of customers stays a focal concern. Liberation shouldn't think twice about privileges or open them to unjustifiable dangers.

Public Products: Certain areas, similar to instruction and medical care, include the arrangement of public merchandise where government mediation might be critical.

Development and Contest: While liberation can encourage advancement, it should not prompt anticompetitive practices or the centralization of force among a couple of predominant players.

Money related Steadiness: Financial strategy, as a type of guideline, assumes a vital part in keeping up with monetary solidness and tending to expansion.

Natural and Social Effect: Liberation, especially in businesses with critical ecological and social ramifications, should be drawn nearer with wariness to stay away from negative externalities.

Worldwide Setting: In an interconnected world, liberation and guideline should likewise think about global economic alliance and worldwide market elements.

5.3 Impact of Economic Liberalization

Financial progression is a strategy structure that underscores lessening government mediation in monetary exercises, advancing business sector driven rivalry, and working with worldwide exchange. It has been embraced by various nations all over the planet, with fluctuating levels of progress and results. The effect of financial advancement is complex, influencing different parts of the economy, society, and administration.

Financial Development and Productivity:

One of the main effects of financial advancement is invigorating monetary development and efficiency potential. By diminishing government limitations and obstructions to showcase section, advancement energizes contest, development, and business. This frequently prompts higher efficiency, expanded venture, and generally financial extension. Nations that have embraced monetary advancement have seen quicker financial development and advancement, which can convert into worked on expectations for everyday comforts for their residents.

Exchange and Worldwide Reconciliation:

Financial advancement is intently attached to expanded exchange and worldwide joining. As boundaries to worldwide exchange are brought down, nations become more associated with the worldwide economy. This can prompt more prominent admittance to unfamiliar business sectors for their items and administrations, working with trades and financial enhancement. Cooperation in worldwide exchange can help a country's monetary possibilities and set out open doors for organizations and shoppers. Be that as it may, it can likewise open homegrown ventures to worldwide rivalry, requiring changes and variations.

Unfamiliar Direct Speculation (FDI):

Monetary progression frequently draws in unfamiliar direct venture (FDI) by establishing a business-accommodating climate. FDI can get capital, innovation, and ability, which can drive financial development and occupation creation.

Drawing in FDI is a vital objective for nations seeking after progression strategies, as it can give the impulse to growing enterprises, further developing foundation, and upgrading the general venture environment.

Pay Disparity:

While financial progression can invigorate generally monetary development, it can likewise intensify pay imbalance inside a general public. The individuals who are better situated to make the most of the new financial open doors might benefit excessively, while underestimated or less-talented portions of the populace might battle to keep up. Tending to pay disparity is a huge test in nations chasing after progression, and social security nets and comprehensive strategies are fundamental to moderating its adverse consequence.

Market Insecurity:

Monetary advancement can prompt market precariousness, especially in the monetary area. Decreasing guidelines can make conditions for speculative way of behaving, bubbles, and monetary emergencies. For instance, the worldwide monetary emergency of 2008 featured a portion of the dangers related with an exceptionally liberated monetary area. Viable administrative oversight is essential to keeping up with monetary steadiness and forestalling foundational chances.

Climate and Maintainability:

The quest for financial development and productivity frequently presents difficulties to ecological supportability. Progression can prompt expanded asset double-dealing, contamination, and ecological debasement in the event that satisfactory guidelines are not set up. Offsetting financial improvement with natural supportability is an intricate errand, and nations should execute strategies and guidelines that energize mindful and feasible practices.

Work Freedoms and Working Circumstances:

Monetary progression can impact work freedoms and working circumstances. As contest escalates, organizations might look for cost-cutting measures, once in a while to the detriment of laborers' privileges and work conditions. It is crucial for carry out work regulations and guidelines that safeguard laborers' freedoms, guarantee fair wages, and lay out safe working circumstances.

Public Administrations and Social Government assistance:

The job of the state in offering public types of assistance and social government assistance can move with monetary advancement. Diminished government spending here can prompt worries about the openness and nature of administrations, especially in medical care, training, and social wellbeing nets. Policymakers should work out some kind of harmony between diminishing the monetary weight and guaranteeing that fundamental administrations stay open and reasonable for all residents.

India's modern strategies play had a vital impact in molding the country's financial scene, from its post-freedom time to the current day. These strategies have gone through tremendous changes and moves, mirroring India's progress from an essentially agrarian economy to one that embraces industrialization and financial advancement. In this exhaustive conversation of India's modern strategies, we will investigate the key turns of events, difficulties, and accomplishments that have denoted this excursion.

Post-Freedom India, in 1947, acquired a fundamentally agrarian economy portrayed by far and wide neediness, restricted industrialization, and frontier heritages. The public authority perceived the requirement for fast industrialization to accomplish independence, diminish reliance on imported products, and create business valuable open doors for a quickly developing populace. Thus, a progression of modern strategies were acquainted with advance homegrown enterprises and encourage financial turn of events.

One of the early drives in such manner was the Modern Approach Goal of 1948. It established the groundwork for a blended economy, wherein the confidential area and the public area would coincide, with the state assuming a focal part in essential areas. The public authority intended to safeguard homegrown enterprises through an arrangement of licenses and allows, import controls, and cost controls. The thought was to energize native modern development while restricting the impact of unfamiliar capital.

The Second Five-Year Plan (1956-1961) denoted one more huge move toward India's industrialization process. This plan stressed the advancement of weighty enterprises, like steel, synthetics, and hardware, which were significant for framework improvement. The foundation of the public area behemoth, Steel Authority of India Restricted (SAIL), was one of the conspicuous results of this methodology. The accentuation on open area endeavors (PSUs) was a vital element of India's modern strategies during this period.

The Modern Strategy Goal of 1956 built up the job of the state in modern turn of events. It grouped enterprises into three classifications: the public area, the confidential area, and the joint area (where both public and confidential areas teamed up). The public authority's methodology was pointed toward diminishing differences in riches and pay dissemination and accomplishing a level of independence.

While these strategies had their benefits, they likewise prompted various difficulties. The authorizing framework, expected to manage modern development, frequently brought about postponements and failures. Administrative obstacles and formality were normal, making it challenging for organizations to easily work. Moreover, the emphasis on import replacement, which expected to lessen dependence on unfamiliar merchandise, at times brought about the creation of inferior quality items.

The 1991 financial changes, otherwise called the LPG (Progression, Privatization, and Globalization) changes, introduced another period for India's modern strategies.

The Indian government, drove by then-Money Priest Dr. Manmohan Singh, left on an excursion to change the economy, diminish government control, and advance confidential area investment. This undeniable a huge takeoff from the prior time of state strength.

The advancement of the Indian economy intended to eliminate limitations on exchange, industry, and unfamiliar venture. It supported unfamiliar direct speculation (FDI) and privatization, which opened up different areas, including media communications, protection, and aeronautics, to private players. This change in approach added to expanded rivalry, further developed productivity, and monetary development.

India's Industrial Rise

One of the critical parts of these changes was the destroying of the Permit Raj, a mind boggling arrangement of licenses and guidelines that had smothered business and development. The public authority's push toward market-situated approaches diminished the requirement for modern licenses and worked with the simplicity of carrying on with work.

The time of financial progression in India additionally saw the steady disinvestment of public area endeavors (PSUs). This permitted the public authority to zero in on administration and administrative capabilities while private undertakings took on a more critical job in financial exercises. The privatization of ventures like media communications and carriers prompted superior assistance quality and productivity.

The effect of these changes was especially apparent in the data innovation (IT) and programming administrations industry. India's IT area experienced quick development, turning into a worldwide IT rethinking center point. The country's gifted labor force, joined with the changed business climate, prompted a flood in IT trades and unfamiliar ventures.

While the monetary advancement achieved various advantages, it likewise presented its portion of difficulties. Pay imbalance expanded, with variations among metropolitan and provincial regions and various states. The opening up of the economy presented a few areas to solid worldwide rivalry, which could be hindering to homegrown ventures that were not sufficiently ready for worldwide business sectors. Also, concerns in regards to the assurance of work freedoms and natural guidelines chasing after monetary development arose.

The period following financial progression saw India broadening its modern scene. The nation saw development in areas like drugs, biotechnology, and sustainable power. The Indian drug industry, specifically, took huge steps, turning into a key part in the worldwide market. The area profited from solid licensed innovation securities and a huge, gifted labor force.

In the 21st 100 years, the Indian government sent off the "Make in India" crusade, which planned to help homegrown assembling and draw in unfamiliar speculation. This drive looked to change India into a worldwide assembling center by working on guidelines, further developing foundation, and advancing key areas like aviation, guard, and gadgets.

The execution of the Labor and products Expense (GST) in 2017 addressed a significant change in India's duty structure. The GST brought together the beforehand mind boggling and divided arrangement of state and focal charges, making a more straightforward and worked on charge system. It intended to advance simplicity of carrying on with work and work with the development of merchandise across state borders.

India's modern approaches likewise underscored the advancement of unique financial zones (SEZs) to draw in unfamiliar venture and advance product situated businesses. These zones offered different impetuses, including charge exceptions, to organizations working inside their limits.

With regards to environmentally friendly power, India took huge steps in saddling sun based and wind power. The public authority acquainted different motivations and arrangements with advance clean energy creation, determined to diminish the country's reliance on petroleum products and tending to ecological worries.

While India's modern arrangements have advanced and adjusted to changing financial circumstances, a few difficulties persevere. Foundation advancement, including transportation and coordinated factors, stays a critical region for development. Deficient framework can prevent the productive development of merchandise and increment functional expenses for organizations.

India additionally faces difficulties connected with expertise improvement and training. Spanning the abilities hole and upgrading the employability of its labor force are essential for the supported development of the modern area. Also, the nation needs to address administrative bottlenecks and regulatory obstacles that can dissuade speculations and business extension.

One of the persevering through difficulties in India's modern scene is the issue of work changes. Adjusting the freedoms of laborers with the requirement for business adaptability and efficiency is a perplexing errand. The public authority has been dealing with work regulation changes to figure out some kind of harmony that supports modern development while safeguarding work freedoms.

Ecological maintainability is another squeezing concern. As India makes progress toward financial development, it should likewise address natural difficulties, including air and water contamination, deforestation, and environmental change. Offsetting modern improvement with ecological conservation is a sensitive errand, however one that is fundamental for the drawn out prosperity of the country.

The new "Atmanirbhar Bharat" (Confident India) drive, sent off in 2020, looks to advance confidence and decrease reliance on imports. This drive is important for a more extensive vision to improve the intensity of Indian ventures and support homegrown assembling. It imagines a more vigorous job for India in worldwide stockpile chains.

Chapter 6

Challenges and Setbacks

Difficulties and misfortunes are an unavoidable piece of the human experience. From the second we make our most memorable strides, we experience obstructions that test our versatility, inventiveness, and assurance. Whether on an individual level, inside our networks, or on a worldwide scale, these difficulties shape our personality and impact our advancement. While they can be dampening, they are likewise amazing open doors for development and learning.

On an individual level, we face various difficulties all through our lives. From youth to advanced age, each stage brings its own novel obstacles. As youngsters, we should explore the intricacies of school, social connections, and self-revelation. This frequently includes confronting scholarly difficulties, managing peer pressure, and conquering self-question. Pre-adulthood introduces a time of character development and self-disclosure, where we wrestle with issues of confidence, self-perception, and individual qualities. Youthful adulthood accompanies the obligations of vocation decisions, monetary freedom, and laying out a feeling of direction. As we become older, we go up against the difficulties of keeping up with physical and psychological wellness, adapting to misfortune, and adjusting to evolving conditions.

In connections, challenges frequently spin around correspondence, trust, and split the difference. Whether in fellowships, heartfelt associations, or relational peculiarities, errors and clashes will undoubtedly emerge. These difficulties can strain bonds, however they additionally give an open door to people to figure out how to comprehend and uphold each other. Also, the intricacies of exploring adoration, closeness, and responsibility in heartfelt connections bring their own arrangement of obstacles. These difficulties can prompt self-improvement and more profound associations whenever maneuvered carefully and compassion.

Inside our networks, challenges manifest in different structures. Monetary ab-berations, separation, and social treachery are determined issues that influence numerous people and gatherings. These difficulties can prompt sensations of feebleness and dissatisfaction, yet they additionally motivate aggregate activity and promotion. Networks frequently meet up to address shared concerns, preparing assets and aptitude to track down arrangements. While the street to advance can be long and difficult, the force of networks to impact positive change ought to be considered carefully.

On a more extensive scale, countries and the worldwide local area face difficulties that can have sweeping results. Ecological issues, for example, environmental change, asset exhaustion, and biodiversity misfortune, represent a danger to the planet's future.

These difficulties require worldwide participation and a promise to supportability. Furthermore, political struggles, financial emergencies, and general wellbeing crises, like the Coronavirus pandemic, can upset soundness and disturb lives for a monstrous scope. These difficulties test the limit of states and foundations to answer successfully and address the requirements of their residents.

In the domain of innovation and development, difficulties and mishaps are characteristic for progress. New developments and disclosures frequently face obstruction, incredulity, and unexpected deterrents. The advancement of notable innovations, for example, man-made consciousness and space investigation, has been set apart by disappointments, mishaps, and moral issues. However, these difficulties additionally give important examples and drive further advancement. The versatility of researchers, architects, and business people notwithstanding difficulties adds to the progression of human information and abilities.

In the business world, challenges are a steady presence. New businesses and laid out organizations the same experience obstacles like market contest, financial slumps, and changing customer inclinations. The innovative soul is portrayed by an eagerness to embrace risk and explore the vulnerabilities of the business scene. Fruitful business visionaries view difficulties not as road obstructions but rather as any open doors to adjust, turn, and enhance.

In the domain of medical services, difficulties and misfortunes are a natural piece of clinical examination and practice. The journey to track down solutions for infections, foster new medicines, and further develop patient consideration is laden with hindrances. Clinical preliminaries might yield frustrating outcomes, therapies might make unexpected side impacts, and clinical experts might confront moral situations. By the by, the commitment of scientists and medical care laborers to the prosperity of patients drives progress in medication and clinical innovation.

In the field of schooling, challenges frequently focus on issues of access, quality, and inclusivity. Instructive establishments should wrestle with financial plan limitations, changing educational program prerequisites, and the computerized partition. The Coronavirus pandemic disturbed customary homeroom getting the hang of, featuring the requirement for advancement and versatility in the training area.

While these difficulties can be overwhelming, they likewise present chances to re-examine and further develop the manner in which we teach people in the future.

In the domain of workmanship and culture, challenges are inborn in the innovative strategy. Specialists and makers frequently face dismissal, basic surveys, and monetary shakiness. However, these difficulties are a fundamental piece of the excursion to creative articulation. They rouse specialists to endure, investigate new structures, and push the limits of their specialty. Workmanship, in the entirety of its structures, is a demonstration of the human soul's capacity to rise above difficulties and mishaps.

6.1 Infrastructure Challenges

Framework is the foundation of present day culture, giving the fundamental physical and hierarchical designs and offices required for the working of a local area or country. It envelops a huge swath of frameworks, including transportation organizations, utilities, correspondence frameworks, and public structures. In any case, regardless of its pivotal job, foundation faces various difficulties and misfortunes that can block its turn of events and support.

One of the most squeezing foundation challenges is the requirement for significant venture. Numerous nations, particularly those with maturing framework frameworks, should apportion critical assets to fix and overhaul their offices. The expense of framework advancement can be galactic, and the monetary weight can strain public spending plans. Lacking subsidizing can prompt conceded support, falling apart framework, and the gamble of disastrous disappointments, for example, span implodes or dam breaks.

Another basic test is the rising interest for reasonable and tough foundation. As the world faces the results of environmental change, there is a developing requirement for framework that can endure outrageous climate occasions, adjust to rising ocean levels, and decrease ozone harming substance emanations. This requires retrofitting existing framework as well as planning new ventures in light of maintainability and versatility. Accomplishing these goals frequently includes complex choices in regards to innovation, materials, and arranging, which can be both expensive and tedious.

The intricacy of foundation projects is a significant obstacle to their prosperity. Huge scope tries, like the development of high velocity rail frameworks, air terminals, or savvy urban areas, require coordination among numerous partners, including government organizations, privately owned businesses, and neighborhood networks. Clashing interests, administrative formality, and varying needs can prompt postponements, cost invades, and debates. Exploring these complexities requests compelling task the board, straightforwardness, and coordinated effort.

Framework challenges are not restricted to created nations; they additionally influence arising economies and agricultural countries. In these locales, foundation deficiencies can be considerably more articulated. Lacking admittance to clean water, sterilization, power, and transportation can prevent monetary development and social turn of events. Tending to these difficulties frequently needs worldwide help, creative funding models, and neighborhood limit building.

Transportation foundation is a basic part of current culture, and it faces its novel arrangement of difficulties. Clogged streets, lacking public travel, and obsolete air terminals can hamper financial efficiency and personal satisfaction. Fabricating and extending transportation networks are fundamental, yet they frequently meet obstruction from networks worried about the ecological effect and land use. Adjusting the requirement for transportation foundation with manageability and public acknowledgment is a mind boggling task.

Energy foundation, including power age and dissemination, is basic for present day life. The progress to cleaner energy sources, like environmentally friendly power, is an imperative test to decrease fossil fuel byproducts and battle environmental change. Be that as it may, the combination of environmentally friendly power into the current power lattice isn't without deterrents. Matrix dependability, capacity limit, and the requirement for foundation updates are contemplations in this change. Besides, energy foundation faces network safety dangers, which require consistent carefulness and interest in safety efforts.

The accessibility and nature of water and sterilization framework are significant for general wellbeing and prosperity. Spotless and safe water supplies, as well as legitimate disinfection offices, are fundamental for forestalling sickness and guaranteeing a great of life. Numerous people group overall need admittance to these fundamental administrations, which presents serious wellbeing gambles. Tending to this challenge includes putting resources into water treatment plants, dispersion frameworks, and sterilization foundation, particularly in underserved regions.

Computerized framework, including the web and correspondence organizations, has turned into a foundation of present day culture. The computerized partition, which alludes to the hole in admittance to innovation and high velocity web between various networks, stays a significant test. Guaranteeing all inclusive admittance to reasonable and great computerized framework is fundamental for advancing financial turn of events, schooling, and social network. Also, safeguarding the protection and security of advanced foundation is a continuous test despite digital dangers and information breaks.

Public structures and offices, like schools, emergency clinics, and government workplaces, are basic parts of a practical society. Keeping up with and revamping these designs is a critical test. Maturing structures may not meet current wellbeing and openness principles, prompting expensive retrofits or substitutions. Spending plan imperatives can bring about conceded support, compromising the security and effectiveness of these offices.

Urbanization represents its own arrangement of framework challenges. As additional individuals relocate to urban communities, the interest for lodging, transportation, and public administrations increments. Overseeing metropolitan development and improvement while limiting ecological effect and guaranteeing impartial admittance to assets is a fragile difficult exercise. This frequently requires long haul arranging, brilliant metropolitan plan, and interest out in the open spaces.

6.2 Labor Issues and Struggles

Work issues and battles have been a foundation of cultural elements for quite a long time, addressing the continuous fight for fair wages, safe working circumstances, and laborers' privileges. From the early work developments to the contemporary worldwide labor force, these issues continue to happen, frequently advancing because of changes in the financial, mechanical, and social scenes.

By and large, the battle for laborers' privileges has been one of the most noticeable work battles. The foundation of worker's guilds and the battle for aggregate dealing privileges were crucial minutes in this continuous fight. Laborers battled for fair wages, sensible working hours, and the finish of shifty practices. The battles for kid work regulations, work environment wellbeing principles, and the option to arrange were hard-won fights that fundamentally better working circumstances and nobility for representatives.

Globalization has presented another layer of intricacies to work issues. While it has opened up valuable open doors for exchange and monetary development, it has likewise prompted reevaluating, offshoring, and the ascent of dubious work. Organizations frequently move tasks to nations with settle for less to reduce expenses, bringing about employment misfortunes and descending tension on compensation in additional created economies. This has prompted banters about fair exchange, safeguarding neighborhood enterprises, and guaranteeing that specialists overall are not exposed to uncalled for or hazardous working circumstances.

In the contemporary scene, mechanical headways, especially in computerization and man-made consciousness, present critical difficulties to the workforce. While these advancements increment proficiency and efficiency, they additionally undermine professional stability for some laborers. Certain enterprises face the gamble of occupation dislodging, provoking worries about retraining the labor force and guaranteeing that mechanical headways benefit laborers instead of leaving them jobless or underemployed.

The gig economy, described by transitory and independent work plans, has acquired unmistakable quality lately. While it offers adaptability, it frequently misses the mark on advantages and insurances that customary everyday work gives. Gig laborers ordinarily need professional stability, medical services advantages, and retirement plans. This change in the idea of work has lighted discussions about business freedoms, specialist order, and the requirement for work regulations to adjust to these new types of work.

Wage imbalance stays a tenacious issue in many regions of the planet. The hole between the most elevated and least workers keeps on augmenting, prompting social and financial variations. The battle professionally wage and impartial compensation for all laborers is progressing. Furthermore, orientation and racial pay holes continue, featuring the requirement for more prominent balance in pay and business valuable open doors.

Work environment segregation and provocation are likewise common work issues. Notwithstanding steps made in advancing variety and inclusivity, numerous laborers actually face segregation in light of race, orientation, sexual direction, or handicap. Lewd behavior in the working environment stays a huge concern, prompting developments and strategies pointed toward establishing more secure workplaces and resolving these issues successfully.

Wellbeing and security in the working environment are vital worries for representatives. Dangerous working circumstances, lacking security conventions, and deficient assurances for laborers in high-risk ventures present huge dangers. Endeavors to further develop security guidelines, uphold guidelines, and consider businesses responsible for keeping up with safe working environments are continuous battles in the work scene.

The Coronavirus pandemic featured the weaknesses and imbalances inside the labor force. Fundamental specialists, including medical services laborers, supermarket workers, and conveyance staff, confronted expanded wellbeing dangers and occupation weaknesses. The pandemic uncovered the requirement for satisfactory medical services, paid debilitated leave, and occupation insurances for all laborers, as well as the significance of tending to the advanced gap for remote work availability.

The continuous battle for movement change is one more aspect of work issues. Outsider specialists frequently face double-dealing, low wages, and risky working circumstances because of their legitimate status. Advocates keep on pushing for exhaustive migration arrangements that safeguard the privileges of settler laborers and recognize their commitments to the economy.

Tending to these work issues requires a complete methodology including government strategies, corporate obligation, trade guilds, and social developments. Co-operation among partners is fundamental to guarantee fair wages, safe working circumstances, and equivalent open doors for all specialists. As the idea of work keeps on developing, the continuous battle for work freedoms stays a crucial piece of molding a fair and only society for laborers across the globe.

6.3 Environmental and Sustainability Concerns

Ecological and supportability concerns have become focal issues in the present worldwide talk. With the world confronting the difficulties of environmental change, asset consumption, and natural corruption, people, networks, legislatures, and organizations are progressively perceiving the pressing requirement for reasonable practices and ecological stewardship.

Environmental change is maybe the most squeezing natural worry within recent memory. The aggregation of ozone harming substances in the climate, principally because of human exercises like consuming petroleum products and deforestation, has prompted climbing worldwide temperatures. The outcomes of environmental change incorporate more successive and extreme climate occasions, ocean level ascent, disturbances in biological systems, and dangers to food and water security. Addressing environmental change requires quick and supported endeavors to decrease fossil fuel byproducts, progress to clean energy sources, and adjust to the progressions currently in progress.

The exhaustion of regular assets is another basic issue. Mankind's utilization of assets like freshwater, minerals, and arable land has arrived at impractical levels. Overexploitation can prompt asset shortage, soil debasement, and water deficiencies. Economical asset the board and preservation are fundamental to guarantee that people in the future approach these essential assets.

Biodiversity misfortune is firmly connected to asset consumption and natural surroundings obliteration. The deficiency of plant and creature species not just lessens the assortment of life on The planet yet in addition upsets biological systems and diminishes their flexibility to natural changes. Preservation endeavors, safeguarded regions, and mindful land-use rehearses are essential to alleviate biodiversity misfortune and shield the wellbeing of environments.

Water shortage is a developing concern, influencing both created and creating locales. As populaces develop and enterprises extend, the interest for freshwater assets strengthens. Contamination, over-extraction, and environment related changes undermine the accessibility of clean water. Maintainable water the board rehearses, effective water system strategies, and the insurance of water sources are vital for address this issue.

Squander the board and contamination present critical difficulties to natural and general wellbeing. The age of waste, from plastics to electronic waste, has arrived at amazing levels, and ill-advised removal defiles land and water. Air contamination from modern emanations and vehicular traffic unfavorably affects air quality and human prosperity. Supportable waste decrease, reusing, and contamination control measures are indispensable to relieve these issues.

The quick urbanization of the total populace has made special manageability challenges. Urban communities drink huge measures of assets and energy, produce critical waste, and add to air and water contamination. Feasible metropolitan preparation, productive transportation frameworks, and green structure practices can assist with relieving the natural effect of urbanization and work on the personal satisfaction for city occupants.

Energy creation and utilization are at the center of natural and maintainability concerns. Petroleum products, which have for quite some time been the essential energy source, discharge carbon dioxide and different toxins into the environment. The change to sustainable power sources, for example, sun based, wind, and hydroelectric power, is a vital procedure to diminish ozone depleting substance discharges and advance manageability. Energy effectiveness measures, like superior protection and energy-productive machines, additionally assume a pivotal part in relieving natural effects.

Land use and deforestation have broad ramifications for the climate. The extension of horticulture, metropolitan turn of events, and logging frequently prompts deforestation and environment annihilation.

The deficiency of woodlands decreases biodiversity as well as adds to fossil fuel byproducts. Reasonable land-use rehearses, reforestation endeavors, and the security of regular territories are vital for counter these issues.

The issue of manageability stretches out to food creation and farming. The worldwide food framework faces difficulties connected with abuse of engineered manures, unreasonable land practices, and food squander. Changing to economical cultivating techniques, lessening food squander, and advancing a shift towards plant-based diets can assist with resolving these issues and guarantee food security for a developing worldwide populace.

Natural equity is a critical part of supportability concerns. Powerless and minimized networks frequently bear an unbalanced weight of natural contamination and the results of environmental change. Addressing ecological shameful acts requires fair strategies and admittance to assets that safeguard the privileges and prosperity, everything being equal, no matter what their financial status or area.

Difficulties and mishaps are an inescapable piece of the human experience. They can influence people, networks, and, surprisingly, whole countries. How we answer these difficulties and misfortunes frequently characterizes our personality, shapes our future, and decides our capacity to beat affliction. In this investigation of difficulties and misfortunes, we will dig into different parts of this general human experience, looking at the wellsprings of difficulties, the manners in which they manifest, and the techniques we utilize to explore them.

Difficulties can appear in a large number of structures, and their beginnings are different and complex. Individual difficulties frequently emerge from the intricacies of day to day existence. People might confront monetary difficulties, medical problems, relationship battles, or individual emergencies. These difficulties can be profoundly private, influencing one's close to home and mental prosperity, as well as their capacity to seek after their objectives and yearnings.

One of the most unavoidable difficulties looked by people and social orders is financial difficulty. Monetary difficulties can come from employment cutback, financial downturns, or individual obligation. Such difficulties can prompt monetary precariousness, stress, and a reduced personal satisfaction. Monetary imbalance is really difficult for social orders around the world, as it can bring about abberations in admittance to schooling, medical services, and essential necessities.

Wellbeing challenges are one more typical and profoundly effective type of affliction. Individual medical problems, whether constant or intense, can upset a singular's life and cause physical and close to home affliction. These difficulties can influence the person as well as their friends and family, who might give care and backing. The more extensive test of general wellbeing, including pandemics and the accessibility of medical care assets, has worldwide ramifications, as featured by the Coronavirus pandemic.

Relationship challenges, whether with regards to families, companionships, or heartfelt organizations, are likewise a wellspring of close to home and mental difficulty. These difficulties can emerge from miscommunication, clashes, double-crossing, or the regular development of connections. They frequently require viable correspondence, sympathy, and think twice about explore effectively.

Cultural difficulties envelop more extensive issues that influence networks, locales, or whole countries. These can incorporate political insecurity, social agitation, racial or ethnic pressures, and ecological emergencies. The effect of such difficulties can be sweeping, influencing the prosperity and security of endless people.

One of the most squeezing cultural difficulties is the issue of environmental change and natural corruption. The results of environmental change, including increasing temperatures, outrageous climate occasions, and ocean level ascent, represent a worldwide danger to biological systems, networks, and economies. Tending to this challenge requires worldwide collaboration, reasonable practices, and strategies to lessen ozone depleting substance outflows.

Political difficulties, like contentions, nationwide conflicts, or tyrant rule, can have annihilating ramifications for the impacted populaces. These difficulties can bring about mass relocation, death toll, and the disturbance of day to day existence. Answers for political difficulties frequently include strategic endeavors, harmony dealings, and worldwide mediations.

Another cultural test is that of social disparity and segregation, which influences underestimated networks around the world. Challenges connected with race, orientation, sexual direction, and financial status endure in numerous social orders. The battle for civil rights and equivalent privileges is progressing and requires aggregate activity and strategy changes.

Mishaps are frequently firmly entwined with difficulties, as they address the obstructions, disappointments, or inversions of progress that people and networks face while going up against troublesome conditions. Misfortunes can emerge from individual or outside factors and can intensify the difficulties previously confronted.

In self-improvement and accomplishment, misfortunes are a typical event. Whether in schooling, profession, or individual objectives, people frequently experience deterrents that briefly block their advancement. These difficulties can result from scholastic battles, employment misfortune, business disappointments, or individual slip-ups. Beating difficulties requires versatility, flexibility, and a development mentality, empowering people to gain from their encounters and endure in their interests.

The business world is no more peculiar to misfortunes. Business visionaries and organizations regularly face difficulties connected with market variances, rivalry, and financial slumps. Business misfortunes can bring about monetary misfortunes, cutbacks, and even insolvency. By the by, strong organizations frequently advance and turn to explore testing times effectively.

Worldwide monetary difficulties, like downturns and monetary emergencies, can have expansive ramifications for people and countries. The 2008 monetary emergency, for instance, brought about broad employment misfortunes, dispossessions, and financial insecurity. Legislatures and monetary organizations frequently answer with money related and financial approaches to settle the economy and backing recuperation.

Development and advance frequently include mishaps. Logical examination, for example, is set apart by experimentation, with various analyses that don't yield the ideal outcomes. Thomas Edison, in his quest for the electric light, broadly said, "I have not fizzled. I've recently found 10,000 different ways that won't work." Such misfortunes are an indispensable piece of the logical strategy and the course of disclosure.

In sports and games, difficulties are a typical part of rivalry. Competitors might encounter wounds, losses, or execution levels. Conquering these misfortunes frequently requires assurance, recovery, and a steady group of mentors and medical care experts. Competitors who persist and gain from mishaps can make incredible progress.

Cultural misfortunes can significantly affect the prosperity of networks and countries. Catastrophic events, like quakes, tropical storms, and fierce blazes, can bring about critical misfortunes, causing death toll, obliteration of framework, and removal of populaces. Catastrophe readiness, reaction, and recuperation endeavors are fundamental in moderating the effect of such mishaps.

Struggle and war address the absolute most obliterating cultural mishaps. Furnished clashes can bring about the deficiency of lives, uprooting of millions, and the annihilation of whole areas. Recuperation and compromise endeavors frequently require global collaboration and long haul obligation to reconstructing impacted networks.

The Coronavirus pandemic fills in as a new illustration of a worldwide difficulty with sweeping results. The pandemic upset medical services frameworks, economies, and day to day existence around the world. Legislatures, researchers, and medical services experts have worked indefatigably to answer the emergency, foster immunizations, and execute general wellbeing measures to alleviate the effect of the infection.

The manners by which people and networks answer difficulties and mishaps shift and frequently rely upon the idea of the misfortune and accessible assets. Versatility, flexibility, and a feeling of local area frequently assume essential parts in beating these hindrances.

People frequently utilize different survival methods to address individual difficulties. Looking for help from companions, family, or psychological wellness experts can give close to home help and direction. Taking care of oneself works on, including activity, contemplation, and care, can assist people with overseeing pressure and keep up with their prosperity. At times, treatment and directing might be important to address further mental or personal difficulties.

Networks and states likewise assume a huge part in tending to cultural difficulties and misfortunes. Social security nets, including joblessness advantages and medical care access, can offer help to people during monetary slumps and emergencies. Local area associations, non-legislative associations (NGOs), and volunteers frequently assemble to give help and assets to those impacted by catastrophic events, clashes, or general wellbeing crises.

Worldwide collaboration is fundamental in tending to worldwide difficulties and misfortunes. Cooperative endeavors among countries can give the assets, aptitude, and financing important to answer issues, for example, environmental change, pandemics, and philanthropic emergencies. Multilateral associations, including the Unified Countries and the World Wellbeing Association, assume basic parts in planning worldwide reactions to challenges that rise above borders.

In the domain of business and business venture, development and flexibility are pivotal for beating difficulties. Business visionaries frequently turn and differentiate their organizations because of changing economic situations. Interest in innovative work can prompt advancement arrangements and new open doors. Admittance to monetary help, including investment and awards, can give the fundamental assets to new businesses to explore difficulties.

In the area of science and examination, misfortunes are an intrinsic piece of the logical cycle. Specialists should embrace disappointment as a chance for learning and revelation. Joint effort with friends and admittance to explore financing are fundamental for tending to complex logical difficulties. Logical straightforwardness and companion survey guarantee the believability and legitimacy of examination discoveries.

In sports, competitors and mentors utilize techniques for defeating misfortunes. Injury restoration, sports brain research, and objective setting are normal instruments for competitors trying to recuperate and move along. Flexibility and mental sturdiness assume a vital part in keeping up with inspiration and making progress.

Chapter 7

Technology and Innovation

Innovation and development are main impetuses that have molded the cutting edge world, essentially modifying the manner in which we live, work, and communicate with each other. From the creation of the wheel to the rise of man-made reasoning, the constant walk of mechanical advancement has been a characterizing element of mankind's set of experiences.

The historical backdrop of innovation is a demonstration of human imagination and inventiveness. All through the ages, people have conceived instruments and machines to beat difficulties, upgrade efficiency, and work on the personal satisfaction. The horticultural upheaval, for instance, denoted a urgent defining moment in mankind's set of experiences, as the improvement of cultivating strategies and devices considered the development of harvests and the training of creatures. This development prompted the development of settled networks, the ascent of civic establishments, and critical advances in food creation and excess.

The Modern Upheaval, one more achievement in mechanical progression, achieved automation, large scale manufacturing, and the advancement of steam motors and rail routes. It changed economies, social orders, and work designs, prompting urbanization and the rise of the advanced industrialized world. Be that as it may, it additionally presented difficulties, including unforgiving working circumstances and financial disparities, which ignited work developments and prompted the advancement of work regulations.

In the twentieth 100 years, mechanical advancement advanced quickly at an exceptional speed. The coming of power, media communications, and transportation headways, for example, cars and planes, changed the manner in which individuals lived and associated. The advanced unrest, set apart by the creation of the PC and the web, changed correspondence, business, and regular day to day existence. These forward leaps associated individuals across the globe and prepared for the data age.

In ongoing many years, the ascent of man-made brainpower (man-made intelligence), computerization, and biotechnology has introduced another time of mechanical advancement. Man-made intelligence can possibly alter businesses, from medical services and money to transportation and assembling. Computerization and mechanical technology are reshaping the labor force and changing the idea of work, as machines take on daily schedule and dreary errands. Biotechnology offers open doors for cutting edge medical care arrangements, crop designing, and ecological reclamation. These arising advancements bring both commitment and difficulties, bringing up moral issues, protection concerns, and the requirement for fitting guideline.

The effect of innovation on the labor force is a subject of huge concern. While computerization and artificial intelligence can build efficiency and effectiveness, they additionally bring up issues about work relocation and the eventual fate of work. Some contend that these advances will set out new position open doors, while others dread that they will bring about a huge loss of business. Setting up the labor force for this changing scene includes upskilling and reskilling, as well as tracking down ways of guaranteeing that the advantages of computerization and simulated intelligence are shared impartially.

Developments in medical care innovation have prompted huge enhancements in clinical consideration, from analytic apparatuses and careful procedures to telemedicine and customized medication. The improvement of immunizations, antitoxins, and clinical imaging has reformed general wellbeing and the treatment of infections. Biotechnology can possibly give forward leaps in hereditary qualities, regenerative medication, and the treatment of beforehand serious circumstances. In any case, admittance to cutting edge medical care advancements stays a test in many regions of the planet, featuring differences in worldwide medical care.

The natural effect of innovation and development is a basic worry in the cutting edge time. While innovation can possibly address natural difficulties, for example, environmental change and asset consumption, it can likewise compound them. The consuming of petroleum derivatives for energy, the development of electronic waste, and the natural outcomes of industrialization have all added to biological corruption. Economical innovation arrangements, sustainable power sources, and capable assembling rehearses are fundamental to moderating these difficulties.

Protection and information security are focal worries in the advanced age. The assortment, stockpiling, and sharing of individual data have brought up moral and lawful issues. Guaranteeing that people have command over their information, safeguarding against cyberattacks, and laying out clear guidelines for the utilization of advanced data are essential for keeping up with the trust of the general population in innovation and development.

Moral problems in innovation and advancement are complex. Questions with respect to the utilization of man-made intelligence in direction, hereditary designing, and the advancement of independent weapons require cautious thought of their ethical ramifications. Offsetting innovative progression with moral qualities, basic freedoms, and the benefit of all is an intricate and continuous test.

The democratization of data through the web and advanced media has brought the two open doors and difficulties. While it has empowered more noteworthy admittance to information and worked with worldwide correspondence, it has likewise led to issues of falsehood, online provocation, and the disintegration of security. Shielding the respectability of online spaces and advancing computerized education are fundamental for tackling the positive capability of innovation.

As innovation and development keep on forming our reality, it is vital to encourage capable advancement, moral practices, and evenhanded access. The job of legislatures, organizations, and people in exploring these difficulties can't be undervalued. Policymakers should figure out some kind of harmony between encouraging advancement and safeguarding the public interest. Organizations have an obligation to guarantee moral and economical practices in their tasks. People assume a part in computerized citizenship, dependable utilization, and the interest for straightforwardness and responsibility.

7.1 The Role of Technology in India's Industrial Growth

India's modern development has been fundamentally impacted by the job of innovation. The country's change from an agrarian economy to an expanding modern force to be reckoned with has been driven by mechanical developments that have upset different areas. Innovation plays had an essential impact in impelling India's modern development, encouraging advancement, expanding efficiency, and growing the country's worldwide seriousness.

The data innovation (IT) area has been one of the most unmistakable drivers of India's modern development. The country's ability in programming improvement and IT administrations deserves it the moniker "the Silicon Valley of the East." The IT area has seen momentous development, powered by a talented labor force, lower work costs, and worldwide interest for IT administrations. The product of programming and IT administrations has essentially added to India's monetary development and unfamiliar trade profit.

India's IT industry has been at the front line of innovation reception, embracing patterns, for example, distributed computing, man-made consciousness, and large information examination. The reevaluating model, which interfaces Indian IT organizations with worldwide clients, has advanced to give a variety of administrations, from programming improvement and business process moving to innovative work. This industry has turned into an image of India's innovative ability and worldwide reach, making position, encouraging business, and driving financial development.

Another area where innovation plays had an imperative impact is producing. The "Make in India" crusade, sent off by the Indian government, expects to change the country into a worldwide assembling center point. Innovation has been instrumental in propelling this goal by upgrading efficiency, advancing cycles, and further developing item quality. Robotization and advanced mechanics have been coordinated into assembling activities, empowering more prominent productivity and accuracy. The reception of Industry 4.0 standards, described by the utilization of the Web of Things (IoT), information investigation, and shrewd assembling, is reshaping India's modern scene.

Mechanical progressions have additionally revived the medical care area in India. Telemedicine, remote checking, and advanced wellbeing arrangements have extended admittance to clinical benefits, particularly in provincial and distant regions.

These innovations have empowered medical care experts to analyze and treat patients from a good ways, further developing medical services results and lessening costs. Also, India's drug industry has tackled innovation for innovative work, prompting the creation of reasonable and top notch prescriptions.

Environmentally friendly power is another region where innovation is driving modern development in India. The country's obligation to maintainability and lessening fossil fuel byproducts has prompted huge interests in sustainable power sources, especially sun based and wind power. Mechanical advancements in sunlight based charger productivity and matrix joining have made sustainable power more savvy and available. India has set aggressive focuses for environmentally friendly power limit, making it a forerunner in this area and adding to a greener and more reasonable modern scene.

In farming, innovation can possibly alter India's provincial economy. The reception of accuracy agribusiness methods, for example, drones, sensor-based observing, and information examination, can upgrade crop yields, lessen asset wastage, and work on the livelihoods of ranchers. Admittance to data through portable applications and the web has engaged ranchers with constant climate information, market costs, and best cultivating rehearses. Innovation empowered production network arrangements are additionally assisting ranchers with associating with business sectors and increment their pay.

Web based business has seen hazardous development in India, driven by the rising utilization of cell phones and further developed web network. Innovation has changed the retail business, making it more straightforward for organizations to arrive at clients and for shoppers to get to many items and administrations on the web. Computerized installment frameworks have become more pervasive, giving secure and advantageous exchanges. Internet business stages have set out new open doors for business people and private ventures to extend their span and flourish in the computerized commercial center.

In the schooling area, innovation has turned into an impetus for mastering and expertise improvement. The multiplication of online courses, e-learning stages, and computerized instructive assets has widened admittance to quality training. This is particularly significant in a country as tremendous and various as India. Innovation has spanned instructive holes, empowering understudies from distant regions to get to instructive substance and associate with instructors. India's edtech industry is quickly developing, offering creative answers for both formal and casual learning.

While innovation has carried various advantages to India's modern development, it has likewise presented specific difficulties. The computerized partition, which remembers variations for web access, computerized education, and mechanical foundation, stays a critical issue. Addressing this hole is fundamental to guaranteeing that the advantages of innovation are available to all portions of society. Furthermore, concerns connected with information protection, network safety, and the moral utilization of innovation should be painstakingly made due.

7.2 Industry 4.0: A Look at High-Tech Sectors

The idea of Industry 4.0, frequently alluded to as the Fourth Modern Transformation, is changing the scene of innovative areas across the globe. Portrayed by the combination of trend setting innovations, information driven cycles, and mechanization, Industry 4.0 addresses another period of modern creation and development. In this article, we will investigate the effect of Industry 4.0 on different cutting edge areas, including producing, medical services, aviation, and planned operations.

Producing, as one of the basic innovative areas, has been at the cutting edge of the Business 4.0 transformation. The reception of advancements like the Web of Things (IoT), man-made consciousness (artificial intelligence), and AI has prompted the making of shrewd production lines. These plants are outfitted with interconnected sensors and gadgets that gather and dissect continuous information. This information driven approach empowers makers to screen the situation with gear, enhance creation processes, and anticipate support needs. With the mix of advanced mechanics and computerization, manufacturing plants can deliver merchandise all the more productively and with higher accuracy. Moreover, 3D printing has arisen as a progressive innovation in assembling, considering quick prototyping and customization.

In the medical care area, Industry 4.0 is achieving huge headways. The assortment and examination of patient information through wearable gadgets, electronic wellbeing records, and telemedicine have empowered medical care experts to go with additional educated choices. Computer based intelligence and AI calculations help with diagnosing illnesses and foreseeing patient results. The advancement of automated a medical procedure frameworks upgrades careful accuracy and negligibly intrusive strategies. Additionally, the utilization of 3D imprinting in medical care considers the making of patient-explicit inserts and prosthetics.

The assembly of these innovations is adding to customized medication and worked on understanding consideration.

The aeronautic trade is another cutting edge area that has embraced Industry 4.0. Airplane makers are utilizing progressed materials and 3D printing to deliver lightweight and eco-friendly parts. IoT sensors and information examination are utilized for continuous observing of airplane wellbeing and execution. Computer based intelligence driven prescient upkeep assists aircrafts with lessening margin time and guarantee security. Furthermore, the advancement of independent robots and air taxis is not too far off, opening up additional opportunities for transportation and operations. The aviation area's coordination of state of the art advances is reshaping the eventual fate of air travel and space investigation.

In the planned operations area, Industry 4.0 is altering production network the executives. The utilization of IoT sensors and RFID innovation gives ongoing perceivability into the development of products. Computer based intelligence and AI calculations upgrade course arranging and freight assignment, diminishing transportation costs and natural effect. Mechanical technology and mechanization are utilized in stockrooms for proficient request satisfaction.

Blockchain innovation is improving straightforwardness and security in supply chains by giving a permanent record to following products. Online business organizations are exploring different avenues regarding drone and independent vehicle conveyances, making the last mile of the store network more proficient. The strategies business is turning out to be progressively spry and receptive to customer requests.

The energy area is going through a change with the reception of Industry 4.0 innovations. Savvy lattices, empowered by IoT gadgets and information examination, upgrade the circulation of power and further develop matrix strength. Environmentally friendly power sources, like breeze and sunlight based, are incorporated with energy capacity frameworks and request reaction instruments to upgrade the dependability and maintainability of energy creation. AI calculations are utilized to anticipate energy utilization designs and change supply likewise. Additionally, the advancement of electric vehicles and their incorporation with the lattice is setting out open doors for more productive and maintainable transportation.

In the domain of horticulture, Industry 4.0 is driving the idea of savvy cultivating or accuracy farming. IoT sensors, robots, and satellite symbolism are utilized to screen crop conditions and assemble information on soil quality. AI calculations break down this information to give experiences into crop the board, bother control, and water system. Computerized farm haulers and robots are sent for planting and reaping. These progressions further develop crop yields, diminish asset utilization, and add to supportable cultivating rehearses.

The development business isn't safe to the impact of Industry 4.0. Building data displaying (BIM) is utilized for cooperative task the executives and plan. 3D printing innovation is utilized to make development parts nearby, lessening burn through and development time. Advanced mechanics and computerization are utilized for undertakings, for example, bricklaying and cement pouring. IoT gadgets are coordinated into structures for shrewd administration of warming, ventilation, and lighting frameworks. The development area is seeing a change that stresses proficiency, manageability, and cost-viability.

The effect of Industry 4.0 isn't restricted to these super advanced areas alone; it stretches out to different spaces, including money, retail, and instruction. Monetary foundations use simulated intelligence and AI to recognize misrepresentation, dissect market drifts, and offer customized monetary types of assistance. In the retail area, information examination and IoT gadgets are utilized to figure out purchaser conduct and enhance stock administration. Instructive organizations consolidate internet learning stages and versatile innovations to upgrade the nature of training and make learning more available.

Notwithstanding the promising headways worked with by Industry 4.0, there are difficulties and contemplations that should be tended to. Information protection and security are vital worries, particularly as the assortment and examination of information become more pervasive. Moral contemplations connected with man-made intelligence and mechanization, like work dislodging, algorithmic inclination, and responsibility, need cautious consideration.

Furthermore, there is a requirement for framework improvement and computerized consideration to guarantee that the advantages of Industry 4.0 are open to all fragments of society.

7.3 Innovations and Their Impact on Industries

Developments have been instrumental in forming the scene of different ventures, driving advancement, improving effectiveness, and changing the manner in which organizations work. The effect of development is expansive, affecting areas going from medical services and transportation to fund and agribusiness. In this article, we will investigate the job of advancements and their significant consequences for these enterprises.

The medical services industry is one of the most powerful areas affected by developments. Clinical forward leaps, mechanical headways, and information driven approaches have altered patient consideration and treatment. Telemedicine, for instance, has made medical services more open, permitting patients to remotely talk with medical services experts. Man-made reasoning (artificial intelligence) and AI are helping with the conclusion of illnesses, the disclosure of new medications, and the personalization of treatment plans. Clinical gadgets, like wearable wellbeing trackers and implantable sensors, are persistently checking patient wellbeing, giving constant information to the two patients and medical care suppliers. The advancement of quality altering innovations, as CRISPR, is opening additional opportunities for the treatment of hereditary problems. These developments are prompting further developed medical care results, cost decrease, and upgraded patient encounters.

In the transportation business, developments are driving tremendous changes in the manner in which individuals and merchandise move starting with one spot then onto the next. Electric vehicles (EVs) are turning out to be more pervasive, lessening ozone depleting substance discharges and reliance on petroleum products. Independent vehicles, furnished with artificial intelligence and sensors, can possibly upgrade street wellbeing and reform the idea of portability. Ride-sharing and on-request transportation administrations have disturbed conventional taxi and vehicle rental ventures, making transportation more advantageous and proficient. High velocity rail and hyperloop innovations vow to reform really long travel, decreasing travel times and natural effect. Developments in avionics, like supersonic flight and electric airplane, are forming the eventual fate of air travel. The transportation area is adjusting to these developments, holding back nothing, and further developed portability.

The money area has seen critical development, especially in the domain of monetary innovation, or fintech. Computerized installment frameworks, portable banking applications, and blockchain innovation have changed how monetary exchanges are led. Digital forms of money, as Bitcoin, are offering options in contrast to customary cash frameworks, rocking the boat of focal banking. Robo-consultants, fueled by computer based intelligence, give mechanized and financially savvy speculation guidance. Crowdfunding stages have democratized admittance to capital for business people and independent ventures.

The use of huge information and AI calculations in monetary examination is improving gamble evaluation, extortion recognition, and exchanging procedures. These advancements are encouraging monetary consideration, smoothing out processes, and expanding openness to monetary administrations.

Farming, frequently thought to be perhaps of the most established industry, is going through a mechanical change. Accuracy horticulture, empowered by IoT gadgets, robots, and information investigation, is enhancing crop the executives and asset use. Independent farm trucks and robots are performing errands like planting and collecting with accuracy and productivity. Genomic advancements and quality altering are propelling harvest reproducing and creature farming, prompting stronger and higher-yielding rural frameworks. Vertical cultivating and aqua-farming are rethinking the idea of customary cultivating, considering all year crop creation in controlled conditions. These advancements are tending to the difficulties of food security, asset protection, and economical farming.

Media outlets has likewise seen significant advancements, especially in how content is made, circulated, and consumed. Web-based features have upset conventional TV and film dispersion models, furnishing buyers with on-request happy and customized suggestions. Computer generated reality (VR) and expanded reality

(AR) advancements are fundamentally altering the manner in which crowds co-operate with amusement, offering vivid encounters in gaming, narrating, and live occasions. Man-made intelligence driven content proposal calculations are fitting substance to individual inclinations, further developing the general client experience. The gaming business has embraced cloud gaming administrations, permitting gamers to stream games on various gadgets. These developments have reshaped the diversion scene, making content more available, drawing in, and intuitive.

The energy area is amidst a change driven by developments in environmentally friendly power innovations. Sun oriented and wind power have become more financially savvy and adaptable, prompting expanded reception and decreased dependence on petroleum products. Energy capacity arrangements, like high level batteries, are tending to the irregular idea of sustainable power sources, guaranteeing a steady and dependable energy supply. Brilliant lattices, controlled by IoT gadgets and information investigation, are working on the administration of energy appropriation and utilization. Developments in thermal power, as cutting edge reactor plans and combination research, offer the potential for cleaner and more bountiful energy sources. These developments are tending to the basic requirement for manageable energy creation and diminishing the carbon impression.

The retail business has been formed by advancements in internet business and store network the board. Online commercial centers and computerized retail facades have changed the manner in which purchasers shop, offering comfort and a more extensive scope of items. Man-made intelligence driven personalization and suggestion motors are upgrading the internet shopping experience, expanding consumer loyalty and reliability.

Advanced mechanics and robotization are being utilized in stockrooms and satisfaction communities for effective request handling. Drones and independent vehicles are being investigated for last-mile conveyance arrangements. Retailers are coordinating innovation to smooth out stock administration and give ongoing bits of knowledge into client inclinations. These developments are rethinking the shopping experience and reshaping the retail scene.

The effect of advancements stretches out to different enterprises, like instruction, land, and assembling. In training, web based learning stages and computerized assets are democratizing admittance to information and upgrading the nature of schooling. Land innovation, or proptech, is altering property the board, development, and the land exchange process. Developments in assembling, including added substance fabricating (3D printing) and robotization, are expanding productivity, diminishing waste, and advancing supportable creation.

While advancements have achieved various advantages to these ventures, they have likewise presented difficulties and contemplations. Information protection and security are vital worries, particularly as the assortment and investigation of information become more predominant. Moral contemplations connected with man-made intelligence and robotization, like work relocation, algorithmic predisposition, and responsibility, need cautious consideration. Furthermore, there is a requirement for foundation improvement and computerized consideration to guarantee that the advantages of developments are open to all sections of society.

Innovation and development have consistently assumed a vital part in forming the course of mankind's set of experiences. From the creation of the wheel to the advancement of the web, these powers have persistently determined progress, changed businesses, and upset the manner in which we live, work, and convey. In this short, we will investigate the powerful connection among innovation and development, looking at their association, influence on society, and potential for future progressions.

The cooperative energy among innovation and development is certain. Development frequently depends on progresses in innovation, and innovation, thus, is driven by imaginative thoughts. This cooperative relationship has pushed human progress forward for a really long time. Mechanical progressions set out new open doors for advancement by giving devices and stages that empower inventive reasoning. For instance, the creation of the print machine in the fifteenth century made ready for progressive improvements in writing, schooling, and correspondence, lighting a flood of imaginative thoughts. Also, the present computerized advancements support development in regions like man-made consciousness, biotechnology, and environmentally friendly power, offering new roads for tending to complex difficulties.

The effect of innovation and development on society is significant. They impact the manner in which we live, work, and connect with our general surroundings. The Modern Upset, for example, introduced a period of innovative advancement that changed assembling, transportation, and farming. This shift prompted urbanization, changed social designs, and worked on expectations for everyday comforts for some.

Moreover, the advanced unrest of the late twentieth 100 years and the 21st century has reshaped how we interface, access data, and direct business. The multiplication of cell phones and the web has made the world more interconnected, empowering extraordinary worldwide correspondence and admittance to information.

Development isn't bound to the domain of business and industry; it reaches out to government, medical services, schooling, and endless different areas. State run administrations advance by creating arrangements and foundation that can bridle innovation to support their residents. Brilliant urban communities, for instance, use innovation to improve metropolitan living, offering effective transportation, squander the executives, and energy arrangements. In medical care, mechanical developments like telemedicine and accuracy medication are working on tolerant consideration and finding. The instruction area has seen a change through internet learning stages and versatile learning innovations, making training more open and customized. Advancements here can possibly address basic cultural difficulties and work on personal satisfaction.

Be that as it may, innovation and development likewise bring difficulties and concerns. The quick speed of mechanical headway can prompt work removal and monetary disturbance. Computerization and man-made brainpower, for example, undermine specific work areas, bringing up issues about the eventual fate of work and the requirement for reskilling and upskilling. Protection and security concerns emerge as computerized innovations gather and offer tremendous measures of individual information. Advancement frequently outperforms the improvement of administrative systems, leaving a hole in resolving these issues. Moreover, the advanced gap, where not all people have equivalent admittance to innovation and its advantages, fuels social and monetary imbalances.

In spite of these difficulties, the potential for future headways in innovation and development is enormous. Arising fields, for example, quantum processing, sustainable power, and biotechnology hold guarantee for addressing a portion of mankind's most squeezing issues. Quantum figuring can possibly upset information handling, making complex computations and reenactments more open, which can prompt headways in materials science, cryptography, and medication revelation. Sustainable power advances, for example, sun oriented and wind power, are vital for tending to environmental change and lessening our dependence on petroleum derivatives. Biotechnology offers open doors for leap forwards in medical services, agribusiness, and natural protection.

Development frequently flourishes in biological systems where cooperation and information sharing are energized. Colleges, research organizations, and organizations cooperate to cultivate inventiveness and critical thinking. Open-source programming and open-access research distributions work with the sharing of information and the cooperative improvement of innovation. Moreover, public-private organizations can use assets and ability from different areas to drive advancement in regions like space investigation and framework improvement.

The job of government in cultivating innovation and development couldn't possibly be more significant. Policymakers can establish a climate that boosts innovative work by offering charge impetuses, awards, and licensed innovation assurances. They can likewise direct enterprises to guarantee that innovative progressions benefit society while protecting against possible damages. Government interest in basic foundation, like broadband organizations, transportation frameworks, and examination offices, can likewise uphold development. Moreover, training and labor force improvement projects can assist with getting ready people for the developing position market, guaranteeing that they have what it takes expected to flourish in an innovation driven world.

One region where innovation and development are particularly critical is medical services. The Coronavirus pandemic featured the significance of advancement in antibody improvement, demonstrative testing, and telehealth. The quick advancement of numerous immunizations in record time exhibits the force of logical development and cooperation. Telehealth, empowered by advanced innovation, has permitted patients to get to clinical consideration from a distance, decreasing the gamble of disease and expanding medical services openness. Besides, information driven approaches in medical services, for example, man-made reasoning and accuracy medication, hold the possibility to change patient consideration by fitting therapies to individual hereditary and clinical attributes.

The eventual fate of transportation is likewise ready for critical advancement. Electric and independent vehicles are set to change the manner in which we move individuals and products. Electric vehicles offer a more supportable and harmless to the ecosystem option in contrast to customary gas powered motor vehicles. In the interim, independent vehicles can possibly make transportation more secure and more effective by lessening human blunder and further developing traffic stream. The blend of electric and independent advancements could reshape metropolitan preparation and decrease blockage and contamination in urban communities.

In the domain of room investigation, innovation and advancement keep on pushing the limits of human accomplishment. Privately owned businesses, as SpaceX and Blue Beginning, are spearheading new ways to deal with space travel, fully intent on empowering interplanetary colonization and asset extraction. Headways in rocket innovation, life emotionally supportive networks, and materials science are making these aggressive objectives more achievable. Besides, the potential for space-based sun oriented power age offers a supportable and basically limitless energy hotspot for Earth.

Man-made reasoning (computer based intelligence) is another field that holds incredible commitment and brings up huge moral issues. Simulated intelligence can possibly upset enterprises, from medical services and money to transportation and amusement. AI and profound learning calculations are driving leap forwards in regular language handling, PC vision, and proposal frameworks. Be that as it may, moral worries encompassing predisposition in computer based intelligence calculations, protection infringement, and the potential for work uprooting request cautious thought and guideline.

The combination of innovation and development is additionally changing the manner in which we produce and consume energy. Environmentally friendly power sources, for example, sun oriented, wind, and hydropower, are progressively supplanting petroleum derivatives. Energy capacity innovations, as cutting edge batteries, empower us to store abundance environmentally friendly power for use when the sun isn't sparkling or the breeze isn't blowing. This shift toward clean energy is fundamental for fighting environmental change and diminishing our reliance on limited petroleum product assets. Besides, the advancement of shrewd matrices and energy the board frameworks considers more effective energy dispersion and utilization.

In the domain of computerized reasoning and AI, advancement is growing the limits of what's conceivable. Computer based intelligence is progressively being utilized for errands like normal language handling, picture and discourse acknowledgment, and independent direction. This has wide applications, from virtual individual aides like Siri and Alexa to independent vehicles and medical care diagnostics. As man-made intelligence calculations become more complex, their expected effect on a large number of businesses, from money and medical services to diversion and transportation, keeps on developing.

Chapter 8

The Future of Indian Industry

The eventual fate of Indian industry holds commitment and presents a scene of chances and difficulties. As India keeps on developing as a worldwide monetary player, a few key elements will shape the direction of its businesses, from assembling and innovation to medical care and environmentally friendly power.

Assembling and Industry 4.0

The assembling area in India is set to encounter a change with the coming of Industry 4.0. The reconciliation of cutting edge innovations, information driven cycles, and computerization is reshaping how items are made. Brilliant processing plants, furnished with Web of Things (IoT) sensors and continuous information examination, are improving efficiency and proficiency. Mechanization, advanced mechanics, and 3D printing are altering creation processes, prompting higher accuracy and adaptability. India is turning into a center point for computerized fabricating, drawing in speculations and cultivating development in the area.

Innovation and Development

Innovation will stay a main impetus behind India's modern future. The data innovation (IT) area, frequently alluded to as India's lead industry, will keep on flourishing, filling in as a worldwide IT reevaluating center. Nonetheless, the scene is developing with a developing spotlight on computerized change, distributed computing, and man-made consciousness. Indian new companies are progressively adding to advancement in regions, for example, fintech, healthtech, and edtech, setting out new open doors and upper hands.

The digitalization of administrations, web based business, and online commercial centers will keep on upsetting conventional plans of action. Versatile web infiltration, combined with reasonable cell phones, is extending admittance to computerized administrations and prodding internet business development. The reception of computerized installment frameworks, contactless exchanges, and blockchain innovation is making a credit only economy. Innovation driven arrangements in coordinated operations, store network the board, and transportation are expanding productivity and lessening costs.

Medical services and Drug Industry

The medical services and drug industry in India is ready for critical development. The country's drug area has been a vital participant in worldwide medication assembling, and India is supposed to proceed with its initiative in the creation of nonexclusive meds. The improvement of biosimilars and antibodies, especially because of the worldwide wellbeing challenges like Coronavirus, will drive development and seriousness in the drug business.

Telemedicine, telehealth, and far off quiet checking are growing admittance to medical care administrations, especially in underserved regions. Man-made consciousness is supporting infection determination and treatment arranging. The emphasis on preventive medical services, healthtech new businesses, and the combination of wearable gadgets into patient consideration are meaningfully having an impact on how medical care is conveyed. The business is likewise encountering a convergence of speculations and organizations in innovative work, setting out open doors for India to arise as a worldwide medical care development center.

Environmentally friendly power and Manageability

As the world movements towards manageable practices, the environmentally friendly power area in India is set to assume a significant part in the country's modern future. India has aggressive objectives for expanding its sustainable power limit, with a solid spotlight on sun based and wind power. The reception of trend setting innovations, like high-productivity sunlight powered chargers and framework mix arrangements, is making environmentally friendly power sources more solid and practical. Energy capacity innovations, as cutting edge batteries, are tending to the discontinuity of sustainable sources, giving a steady energy supply.

Brilliant network frameworks, empowered by IoT gadgets and information investigation, are working on the administration of energy circulation and utilization. The joining of electric vehicles and the improvement of charging framework are adding to a cleaner and more supportable transportation area. India's environmentally friendly power drives are decreasing fossil fuel byproducts as well as encouraging mechanical development and occupation creation.

Aviation and Protection

India's aviation and guard businesses are ready for development and modernization. The guard area is zeroing in on native assembling and innovative work to decrease reliance on imports. The "Make in India" crusade expects to support homegrown creation of protection gear, prompting joint efforts with worldwide safeguard producers. The aeronautic trade is encountering progressions in airplane fabricating, drone innovation, and space investigation. The improvement of provincial air availability and the development of private space organizations are opening new wildernesses in the aviation area.

Farming and Food Handling

The farming and food handling industry in India is going through a computerized upset. Accuracy horticulture, driven by IoT gadgets, information examination, and man-made intelligence, is streamlining crop the executives and asset use. Robotization in cultivating processes, including the utilization of independent farm trucks and robots, is expanding effectiveness and harvest yields. The improvement of hereditarily adjusted crops and imaginative cultivating rehearses is tending to food security challenges. Economical horticulture, natural cultivating, and vertical cultivating are arising patterns. The food handling area is utilizing innovation to further develop sanitation, lessen waste, and upgrade item quality.

Difficulties and Contemplations

While the eventual fate of Indian industry is promising, it isn't without difficulties and contemplations. Tending to the advanced separation and guaranteeing computerized proficiency are critical for impartial admittance to the advantages of innovation. Online protection dangers and information security concerns should be overseen really to keep up with trust in advanced frameworks. Moral contemplations connected with simulated intelligence, mechanization, and occupation dislodging require smart strategies and guidelines. Foundation advancement, especially in rustic regions, is vital for help the development of innovation driven enterprises.

Reasonable practices, natural protection, and mindful asset the board will be integral to India's modern future. Offsetting financial development with natural obligation is a complicated undertaking that requires inventive arrangements and administrative systems.

The requirement for a gifted labor force to help the developing ventures couldn't possibly be more significant. Interest in schooling, professional preparation, and reskilling programs is fundamental to guarantee that the workforce is prepared to satisfy the needs of arising cutting edge areas. Cooperation between industry, the scholarly world, and government is vital to cultivating advancement and innovative work.

8.1 India's Aspirations in Key Sectors

India, with its huge and various scene, is trying to arrive at new levels across key areas, driven by monetary development, mechanical progressions, and an emphasis on supportability. These desires are obvious in areas like assembling, innovation, medical services, environmentally friendly power, aviation, horticulture, and training, every one of which assumes an essential part in forming the country's future.

Fabricating:

India's assembling area is on a groundbreaking excursion, planning to accomplish independence, worldwide intensity, and financial development. The "Make in India" drive, sent off by the public authority, tries to lay out India as a worldwide assembling center point. The country's emphasis is on expanding the commitment of assembling to Gross domestic product, improving efficiency, and setting out work open doors.

The reception of Industry 4.0 standards, described by the joining of trend setting innovations, information driven cycles, and robotization, is reshaping Indian assembling. Shrewd processing plants, outfitted with the Web of Things (IoT) sensors and constant information investigation, are improving creation proficiency and item quality. Computerization and advanced mechanics are reforming producing processes, lessening work concentrated undertakings, and further developing accuracy.

India is situating itself as a center point for computerized fabricating, with a developing accentuation on 3D printing, which is making quick prototyping and customization more open.

Furthermore, the "Aatmanirbhar Bharat" (confident India) drive is driving independence in basic areas, like protection and medical care, by advancing home-grown assembling and innovative work.

Innovation:

The innovation area in India has for quite some time been known for its ability in programming administrations, IT rethinking, and advancement. India's goals in this area are to outfit advanced change, man-made consciousness, and arising advancements to encourage development, increment worldwide seriousness, and drive monetary development.

India's flourishing startup environment is a demonstration of its innovation desires. The nation is home to a blossoming number of new businesses that are transforming different spaces, including fintech, healthtech, edtech, and agritech. These new companies are making inventive arrangements as well as drawing in ventures and cultivating business.

The digitalization of administrations, internet business, and online commercial centers is significantly having an impact on how business is led. Versatile web infiltration and the reasonableness of cell phones are extending admittance to advanced administrations, prodding web based business development. Computerized installment frameworks, blockchain innovation, and contactless exchanges are making India's progress to a credit only economy a reality.

Furthermore, the reception of distributed computing, large information investigation, and simulated intelligence is changing the manner in which organizations work, making them more proficient, client driven, and around the world cutthroat. India's IT and innovation area is ready to assume a basic part in the worldwide computerized economy, as well as in tending to homegrown difficulties in regions like medical services and farming.

Medical services:

India's medical services desires are centered around further developing medical care access, quality, and reasonableness. Telemedicine, telehealth, and distant patient observing are extending medical care administrations to remote and underserved regions. The Coronavirus pandemic sped up the reception of telemedicine, making medical services discussions more helpful and available. Man-made brainpower and AI calculations are helping with sickness analysis, anticipating patient results, and medication revelation. The improvement of automated a medical procedure frameworks is upgrading careful accuracy and negligibly obtrusive systems.

Moreover, India's drug industry is a worldwide forerunner in the creation of nonexclusive meds. The country's desires in this area are to keep creating biosimilars and immunizations, particularly because of worldwide wellbeing challenges like the Coronavirus pandemic.

The combination of wearable gadgets and the web of clinical things (IoMT) is making medical services more persistent driven, empowering constant checking and information driven therapy.

The emphasis on preventive medical care and wellbeing is acquiring unmistakable quality, prompting a more noteworthy accentuation on wellness innovation and computerized wellbeing arrangements. The joining of wearable gadgets into medical services isn't just upsetting patient consideration but at the same time is setting out open doors for healthtech new companies and exploration.

Environmentally friendly power:

India's environmentally friendly power yearnings are interlaced with its obligation to supportability and decreasing fossil fuel byproducts. Sun based and wind power have become more financially savvy and versatile, making India a forerunner in the reception of sustainable power sources. The country has set aggressive focuses for expanding its sustainable power limit, with an emphasis on sunlight based and wind power.

The improvement of energy stockpiling arrangements, like high level batteries, is tending to the discontinuous idea of environmentally friendly power sources, guaranteeing a steady energy supply. Shrewd frameworks, controlled by IoT gadgets and information investigation, are working on the administration of energy conveyance and utilization. The joining of electric vehicles and the improvement of charging framework are adding to a cleaner and more feasible transportation area.

India's environmentally friendly power drives are decreasing fossil fuel byproducts as well as cultivating mechanical advancement and occupation creation. These desires line up with India's obligation to accomplishing its environment objectives and tending to the squeezing worldwide test of environmental change.

Aviation:

The aviation and guard area in India has desires to modernize and turn out to be more confident. The guard area, specifically, is zeroing in on native assembling and innovative work to diminish reliance on imports. The "Make in India" crusade tries to reinforce homegrown creation of protection gear, prompting joint efforts with worldwide guard producers.

In the airplane business, progressions in airplane producing, drone innovation, and space investigation are becoming the overwhelming focus. The advancement of local air network and the development of private space organizations are opening new wildernesses in the area.

India's aviation and protection area's yearnings line up with public safety objectives, mechanical development, and occupation creation. It plans to meet homegrown protection prerequisites as well as turned into a huge player in the worldwide avionic business.

Horticulture:

India's horticulture area plays a pivotal part in the country's goals for food security, asset preservation, and maintainable farming. Accuracy farming, driven by IoT gadgets, information investigation, and simulated intelligence, is improving harvest the executives and asset use. Mechanization in cultivating processes, including the utilization of independent farm trucks and robots, is expanding proficiency and harvest yields.

The advancement of hereditarily changed crops and creative cultivating rehearses is tending to food security challenges. Reasonable agribusiness, natural cultivating, and vertical cultivating are arising patterns. These yearnings line up with the need to guarantee food security for a developing populace and address natural difficulties related with customary cultivating rehearses.

8.2 Sustainable and Inclusive Industrial Growth

Supportable and comprehensive modern development has turned into a basic in this day and age, with a developing accentuation on offsetting monetary improvement with natural obligation and social value. It incorporates the possibility that enterprises can drive financial advancement while limiting their effect on the climate and guaranteeing that the advantages of this development are available to all sections of society. This idea is critical for countries to fabricate strong economies, address worldwide difficulties, and make a superior future for all.

Economical Modern Development:

Maintainability in modern development includes embracing rehearses that limit the exhaustion of regular assets, lessen contamination, and moderate environmental change. Key parts of supportable modern development include:

Environmentally friendly power Reception: Progressing to environmentally friendly power sources, for example, sun based, wind, and hydroelectric power, lessens ozone depleting substance emanations and dependence on petroleum products. This progress isn't just fundamental for moderating environmental change yet additionally for making a more practical energy biological system.

Asset Productivity: Businesses are progressively zeroing in on asset effectiveness, including lessening water utilization, improving energy use, and limiting waste age. Round economy standards, which advance reusing and reusing materials, are acquiring unmistakable quality in different areas.

Supportable Stock Chains: Feasible practices reach out to supply chains, with organizations progressively requesting manageability from their providers. This includes mindful obtaining of natural substances, moral work rehearses, and limiting the ecological effect of coordinated operations and transportation.

Green Advancements: Interests in eco-accommodating innovations, like green framework, electric vehicles, and energy-productive assembling processes, assume a vital part in decreasing the natural impression of ventures.

Ecological Guidelines: States and worldwide bodies are establishing and implementing natural guidelines to urge enterprises to diminish their carbon impression. Emanation decrease targets, carbon evaluating components, and natural consistence guidelines are driving businesses toward manageability.

Comprehensive Modern Development:

Comprehensive modern development centers around guaranteeing that financial improvement helps all citizenry, diminishing imbalances, and advancing social prosperity. Key parts of comprehensive modern development include:

Work Creation: Growing enterprises ought to make occupations that are available to assorted populaces, including underestimated networks and weak gatherings. This can assist with decreasing joblessness and neediness.

Ability Improvement: Giving expertise advancement open doors guarantees that people can take part in and benefit from monetary development. Preparing and schooling programs assist laborers with adjusting to the changing modern scene.

Orientation Inclusivity: Orientation equity is imperative for comprehensive development. Guaranteeing that ladies have equivalent open doors in the labor force, equivalent compensation, and assurance from separation is critical.

Advancement and Business: Empowering development and business venture, particularly among underrepresented networks, cultivates financial development and social versatility. Admittance to financing and assets for new companies and independent ventures is fundamental.

Social Wellbeing Nets: Powerful friendly security nets, including medical care, instruction, and joblessness benefits, are basic to supporting people and families during monetary changes and emergencies.

Local area Advancement: Modern development ought to help the networks in which ventures work. This might include interests in framework, training, and medical services here.

Difficulties and Contemplations:

Accomplishing manageable and comprehensive modern development isn't without its difficulties and contemplations. Here are a few central issues to consider:

Adjusting Monetary Development and Ecological Protection: The quest for financial development can at times struggle with natural preservation endeavors.

Finding some kind of harmony is a complicated undertaking, requiring creative arrangements and viable guidelines.

Energy Change: Progressing to environmentally friendly power sources frequently requires significant ventures and can prompt work dislodging in customary energy areas. Dealing with this change while guaranteeing the prosperity of impacted laborers is a critical test.

Imbalance and Separation: Tending to disparity, segregation, and variations in admittance to open doors is a complex issue. It includes strategy changes, social moves, and designated drives to inspire underestimated gatherings.

Worldwide Collaboration: Accomplishing manageability and inclusivity in modern development is a worldwide exertion. Worldwide participation, arrangements, and shared objectives are fundamental to resolving issues that rise above public limits, for example, environmental change.

Reskilling and Long lasting Learning: The quickly changing modern scene expects laborers to overhaul their abilities ceaselessly. Putting resources into reskilling and deep rooted learning programs is important to guarantee that the labor force stays versatile.

Natural Obligation of Ventures: Enterprises assume a crucial part in ecological protection. Guidelines, motivators, and industry principles are basic to guaranteeing that organizations assume a sense of ownership with their ecological effect.

Social Wellbeing Nets: Creating hearty social security nets can be costly. Subsidizing and guaranteeing the supportability of these projects are basic for supporting people during monetary changes and giving them a wellbeing net in the midst of hardship.

Examples of overcoming adversity:

A few nations and districts are taking critical steps toward feasible and comprehensive modern development. For instance:

The European Association (EU): The EU has carried out strategies and guidelines pointed toward lessening fossil fuel byproducts and advancing manageability. The European Green Arrangement is an aggressive drive that tries to make Europe the world's most memorable environment unbiased mainland by 2050. This includes critical interests in sustainable power, round economy practices, and green advancements.

Scandinavian Nations: Nations like Sweden, Norway, and Denmark are known for their far reaching social wellbeing nets, solid work insurances, and a guarantee to orientation fairness. These countries reliably rank high on worldwide lists of social prosperity and manageability.

Costa Rica: Costa Rica is a perfect representation of a country that has embraced sustainable power sources. The country has been controlled by a blend of hydropower, wind, sun oriented, and geothermal energy, and it tries to become carbon-impartial by 2050.

Rwanda: Rwanda's endeavors to advance inclusivity and ladies' cooperation in the labor force have prompted exceptional advancement. The country has seen an expansion in female portrayal in political and monetary circles and has areas of strength for encountered development.

8.3 India's Role in the Global Industrial Landscape

India's job in the worldwide modern scene is consistently developing, set apart by a developing economy, mechanical headways, and expanding impact in key areas. As one of the world's quickest developing significant economies, India is ready to assume a critical part in molding the worldwide modern scene. Here are a few critical parts of India's job in this unique situation:

Financial Development and Flexibility:

India's supported financial development is one of the focal variables characterizing its spot in the worldwide modern scene. The nation's tremendous and various economy, driven by a youthful labor force and a blossoming working class, has drawn in worldwide consideration. India's monetary versatility, especially despite worldwide financial vulnerabilities, is significant. As the world looks for potential open doors for venture and development, India is an appealing objective.

Mechanical Headways and Development:

India has set up a good foundation for itself as a center point for innovation and development, especially in the data innovation (IT) area. The nation is known for its product administrations, IT re-appropriating, and a flourishing startup environment. Indian tech organizations have a worldwide presence, offering types of assistance and answers for clients around the world. This mechanical ability stretches out to arising innovations like man-made brainpower, blockchain, and advanced change.

Fabricating and Modern Skill:

India's assembling area is going through critical change, with a solid accentuation on drives, for example, "Make in India" and "Aatmanirbhar Bharat" (confident India). The coordination of cutting edge innovations, like Industry 4.0 standards, is reshaping producing cycles and making India a cutthroat player in worldwide stockpile chains. The country's modern ability reaches out to areas like drugs, car, and aviation.

Worldwide Exchange and Unfamiliar Direct Venture:

India's job in the worldwide modern scene is highlighted by its support in global exchange and unfamiliar direct venture (FDI). The country is important for different worldwide and territorial economic alliance, and its FDI approaches have opened ways to unfamiliar financial backers.

India's homegrown market and talented labor force make it an alluring objective for unfamiliar organizations hoping to grow their presence.

Environmentally friendly power and Maintainability:

India is focused on maintainable modern practices and environmentally friendly power reception. The nation is a worldwide forerunner in environmentally friendly power, especially in sun oriented and wind power. These drives line up with worldwide endeavors to battle environmental change and advance natural maintainability.

Worldwide Wellbeing and Drug Creation:

India's drug industry is prestigious for its job in worldwide medical care. The country is a central participant in the creation of nonexclusive drugs, making medical care more reasonable and open around the world. India's drug ability reaches out to the improvement of antibodies and biosimilars, tending to squeezing worldwide wellbeing challenges.

Aviation and Protection:

India's aviation and protection ventures are set apart by advancement and independence drives. The country is putting resources into native assembling and innovative work, lessening reliance on imports. This assumes a part in molding the worldwide aviation and guard scene.

Instruction and Expertise Advancement:

India's job in the worldwide modern scene is likewise characterized by its human resources. The nation is home to a youthful, taught, and talented labor force. Training and expertise advancement programs are getting ready people to fulfill the needs of arising enterprises and take part in the worldwide labor force.

Difficulties and Contemplations:

India's development direction in the worldwide modern scene isn't without challenges. Key contemplations incorporate tending to pay disparity, upgrading framework improvement, and guaranteeing capable modern practices. India should likewise explore international elements and adjust to the changing worldwide exchange climate.